Conquering Dysfunction in the Workplace

Three Winning Strategies to Bring New Life to Troubled Work Environments

by

Barry D. Cooney, Ph.D.

First Edition
Copyright ©2004 Barry Cooney
All rights reserved.

Jade Bear Publications
1704-B Llano Street, Suite 244
Santa Fe, New Mexico 87505
Telephone: 888-474-0515 (toll-free)

Library of Congress Cataloging-in-Publication Data
Library of Congress Control Number: 2004092605
Cooney, Barry, 2004
Conquering Dysfunction in the Workplace:
Three Winning Strategies to Bring New Life
to Troubled Work Environments

ISBN # 0-9753479-0-X

Author contact: bcooney779@aol.com
Telephone: 888-474-0515 (toll-free)

Book design by Melanie Pahlmann

for
Karin

*"Und die Liebe
ist die Luft
die wir trinken."*

Acknowledgements

There are a handful of wonderful people that deserve mention for the kindness, encouragement and guidance they have provided me in the writing of this book. First, a big hug to Melanie Pahlmann who edited the manuscript, designed the cover and made the book print ready. Her meticulous work is much appreciated. Another round of heartfelt thanks goes to Victor la Cerva, John Gervers, David Johnson, Juan Velasco and Walt Schliemann. Each in their own way has provided me with the kind of support that can only come from loving friends; I'm very grateful to have all of them in my life.

I want to further acknowledge two exceptional spiritual teachers: Dr. Rolando Carbonell, from the Philippines, and Joan Halifax Roshi, Abbot and Head Teacher at the Upaya Zen Center in Santa Fe. "Rolly" has encouraged me for years to set down in print my experiences with organizations, while Joan Roshi, by virtue of the loving-kindness that she exudes, has been a real source of inspiration and "quiet mind."

I also want to send prayers of peace to one of my greatest guides, Albert Carlo, known by his intimates as "The Count." Count Carlo has been deceased for some years now, but his mentorship and "joie de vivre" will never be forgotten. It was Carlo who taught me how to move through hardship, and see light in the midst of darkness. His simple adage, "Life Provides" has sustained me through all manner of challenges and obstacles.

Lastly, I owe much to the many hard working, compassionate people that I have met in my various projects over the years. Many of them went unrecognized in their own places of business. Never-the-less, their caring and sacrifice for others makes them heroes in their own right. Their good work will always be remembered.

Barry Cooney
Santa Fe, New Mexico
April 6, 2004

Table of Contents

We shall not cease from exploration,

And the end of all our exploring will be

to arrive where we started, and know

the place for the first time.

~ T.S. Eliot

Introduction

"Dis-ease" is the word I use to talk about dysfunction in business. To me it makes more sense than the word dysfunction, although, at times, I use both words interchangeably. I prefer dis-ease not just because it looks like the word disease, which speaks of illness, but because it seems to be wholly descriptive of the core genesis of organization dysfunction. Troubled businesses are not merely dysfunctional—they are seriously "not at ease." When a business is "at ease" it feels quite comfortable with what it's doing and how it's being done. Dis-eased businesses feel just the opposite. They manifest a kind of entropy that borders on decay. Their deteriorating operations often exist amidst appearances of frenetic, purposeful activity. At best, organizations of this ilk are numbing, at worst, despotic and authoritarian.

I had an early indication of what dis-eased businesses were like from stories told to me by my father. He was employed for many years at a manufacturing plant in the northeastern United States, one that stamped out auto bodies, and railroad car frames. The plant didn't have a terribly good safety record. Every other week I was subjected to another gruesome narrative about a fellow who lost an arm, an eye or several fingers in one of those huge presses. My father believed

The truth does not change

according to our ability to stomach it.

~ Flannery O'Connor

that the company's management exploited its workers. It led him to become active in the local union. By the time I reached high school, he was the union's president.

He was bitter and unhappy about his job. But his strong Irish laborer background—nurtured by the teachings of his father and grandfather, lifelong dockworkers in New York—demanded that he provide well for his family—at whatever emotional or physical cost.

Toward the end of his work career, his bitterness had hardened still further. He continued to believe that management was inherently evil. But now, he also thought ill of the union workers he represented. I asked him about this one day. He sighed deeply and said, "Management wants to get as much out of the working guy as they can, and give him as little in return as they can get away with. By the same token, many of the union guys hardly do any work and ride on the coattails of people who sweat blood to earn a decent living. They use the union as a protective shield so that they can do as little as possible and still get paid." Wearied by these burdensome issues, he took an early retirement. Two years later, he was consumed by cancer and died.

Listening to his experiences of work life left a big impression on me. I wondered about the nature of work. I began to ask a lot of questions: Did work need to be so repressive? Was management always out to exploit workers? What would it take to make a work environment feel purposeful and exciting? How do you motivate people to do a good job?

I've continued to ask myself these questions while following a rather circuitous career path, which included stints as a clinical therapist,

When you're green, you're growing.

When you're ripe, you rot.

~ Ray Kroc

a state government official, a director of a trendy fitness resort, and a producer of a leading chamber orchestra. Finally, I settled down and discovered my true passion—working with people in business. After years of applied effort, in all types of business settings—wearing "Bunny Suits" in clean rooms of computer chip Fabs; crawling down open sewers with street repairmen; in the board rooms of large financial brokerage houses; riding atop hook and ladders with firefighters; behind blackjack pits in opulent casinos—I've been able to develop answers to the more important questions, about dis-ease in business.

I now accept the fact that working in dis-eased places for long periods of time is tantamount to a death of the soul. Even visiting such places can produce a noticeable drop in physical and emotional energy. My first personal encounter with dis-ease in business occurred many years ago when I interviewed for a mid-level management job with the Internal Revenue Service. I flew to Washington, DC from my adopted home in Santa Fe, New Mexico. When I arrived at IRS Headquarters, I was confronted by an enormous cold granite structure. Entering this tomb-like edifice, I was taken aback by the drabness of the setting. The corridors, which appeared to extend to infinity, were painted a dull off white. Evidently, over time, the walls had darkened to the point where they looked dirty and unkempt. I thought for a moment that I was standing in the middle of a large intestine. It was wintertime, and the place was heated—or more accurately speaking—overheated, causing me to feel somewhat sick to my stomach.

The fellow who greeted me, was bland and expressionless. I was led to a small, sparsely furnished office which contained a six foot rectangular steel gray table. Behind the table sat two men. Both wore navy blue suits, which looked like they had been purchased at a discount

Either this man is dead

or my watch has stopped.

~ Groucho Marx

store. The first guy gave me a half smile and extended his hand, giving mine a limp, cursory shake. Everyone then introduced themselves. At that very moment, I had a startling realization: there was no way I could work in this environment. Something about it seemed awkward, unnatural, even diseased! However, since I traveled twelve hundred miles for the interview, I wasn't prepared to leave just yet.

The questions they asked me were all *pro forma*: Why was I interested in the job? Had I ever supervised people? Was I familiar with the way federal government operated? And so on. Eventually we reached the summary question: "Now, Mr. Cooney, do you have any questions for us?" Without a moment's hesitation, "I replied, "Yes, do you know a good Chinese restaurant in the area?"

They gave each other a quizzical look. Then, the guy with the limp handshake said he thought there might be one a few blocks away. He then gave me some awkward sounding directions. We all stood up. They bade me farewell. I did the same, knowing that chances were nil that I would ever return to that intestinal fortress. Armed with what turned out to be the wrong directions, I eventually found the restaurant in question. After eating a plate of fairly decent egg foo young, I caught the afternoon flight back to New Mexico.

I relate this tale only to suggest that one doesn't need to be an expert in organization and management development to be able to "feel" that a work environment is dis-eased. It didn't take long for my intuitive antennae to give me the *feeling* that the I.R.S. was "not the most cutting edge business in the world." If anything, I had a gut impression of a lifeless workplace—one characterized by plodding monotony, hampered at every turn by cumbersome rules and regulations. (I sometimes wonder if those corridors have ever been repainted!)

Advice is what we ask for when we

already know the answer,

but wish we didn't.

~ Erica Jong

Because human beings are creatures of habit, are capable of adapting to many situations, some of which border on the intolerable, we often find ourselves in work settings that are clearly not healthy. You know the kind I'm talking about—ones which drain energy, and give little in return—except the privilege of coming back the next day and repeating everything all over again.

I firmly believe that dysfunctional, dis-eased businesses can be reshaped into energetic, on-purpose, enterprises—ones that are both healthy and profitable. It's because I carry this belief, that I decided to share anecdotes and insights about the phenomenon of dis-ease in the workplace, and, at the same time, outline some specific concepts I've developed to bring about meaningful change in workplace environments.

Part One of this book attempts to develop a clearer understanding of how dysfunctions manifest in work environments, together with the resulting breakdown of on-purpose communication. Part Two identifies *Ten Leadership Characteristics*, the sum of which embodies a strategy for tackling business dysfunction directly through the strength and clarity of its leaders. Part Three details a specific approach to bringing fragmented organizations into alignment by forming "Strategic Partnerships" throughout the enterprise. This approach is designed to work hand and glove with the leadership initiatives contained in Part Two. The Final Part, *A New Look at the Glass Bead Game,* seeks to lay the ground work for businesses to incorporate "focused awareness" practices into their cultures, as a mechanism for enhanced insight about ethics, integrity, and the expanded role of business in a global economy.

As a believer in "Universal Truths," I've peppered the book with quotations of timeless wisdom, with the expectation that the words of

If you don't reveal yourself,

people will invent you and then

you'll have to live with that invention.

~ Anonymous

great thinkers, both past and present, will trigger additional insights about the kind of motivation, courage, positive thinking and sense of humor that is required to make positive change a reality.

The philosopher William James (1842—1910) once noted: "The art of being wise is the art of knowing what to overlook." Much has been intentionally overlooked in this analysis of business dysfunction. I hope that the kernels of thought that are included within these pages produce just enough wisdom for you, the reader, to make a real difference in reshaping your work environments, for both employees and customers alike.

Strong lives are motivated

by dynamic purposes.

~ Kenneth Hildebrand

Part One:

The Anatomy of Dis-eased Businesses

"Everyone and everything around you is your teacher."

~ Ken Keyes, Jr.

Dis-eased businesses are sluggish, short on energy and lack initiative. Like many physical diseases, dis-eased workplaces are harmful to people who reside in them. Dis-eased businesses don't serve the best interests of either their employees or customers. That's because they lack integrity—they simply don't "walk their talk."

Many dis-eased companies are in miserable shape. For example, certain government and non-profit institutions are so unhealthy that they would collapse overnight if their operations weren't buttressed by taxpayer dollars or buoyed up through external contributions. (I refer to these kinds of entities as "Living Dead Organizations" based on the classic horror movie "The Night of the Living Dead," because although they are technically deceased, they function as if they were alive.)

The deepest principle of human nature

is the craving to be appreciated.

~ William James

Dis-eased businesses have patterns of dysfunction that sometimes seem almost hopeless. The presence of one dis-ease factor, say, mistrust, usually indicates the presence of others: poor communication, unclear goals, outdated policies, lack of direction, etc. Basically, dis-ease factors take hold when behaviors and attitudes become corrupted over time because of ineffective leadership.

When leadership fails to identify and correct dysfunctions they turn into full blown dis-ease patterns which spread throughout the workplace, much like cancer cells migrating to other organs. For example, while conducting an assessment of the operations of a large urban Chamber of Commerce, I had occasion to interview various department directors. At some point during each of the interviews, one of the interviewees would inevitably "bad mouth" a colleague. Typically, the group characterized each other as being untrustworthy, incompetent, lazy or opportunistic. It was no surprise to discover that communication within this outfit was in a shambles.

This internal back biting had shattered communication within the larger organization. I soon discovered that each intact service area acted like an island unto itself. Each one reflected a marked disdain for the director, who was, in fact, a fairly nice and well intended fellow. However, in his capacity as director, he was totally indecisive and ineffectual. His anemic leadership style allowed senior managers to run wild with their back biting antics. Because these behaviors were carried out at the senior level, it virtually assured that every point of operational interface would reflect strong patterns of dis-ease.

The Onset of Dis-ease

Consciously or unconsciously, managers greatly influence the thoughts and actions of their subordinates, by virtue of their positions of author-

Help! I'm being held prisoner by my heredity and environment.

~ Dennis Allen

ity and control. When managers are well aligned in their thinking and possess clear, equitable performance standards, they inspire confidence and purpose. However, if managers are not aligned, and operate instead from inconsistent sets of norms and values, fragmentation and disarray set in. Once this occurs, the dis-ease process becomes implanted directly into the company's operational fabric.

This was certainly the case with the Chamber of Commerce I encountered. Through divisiveness, each manager negated whatever leadership potential they had. Each was in service to himself. The company was merely a playing field to serve their own self interests and personal agendas. This scenario delineates our first rule of dysfunction: it begins to manifest as a breakdown of leadership. Note the use of the word "leadership" as opposed to management. The former connotes direction, purpose and intention, the latter handling or controlling.

In the absence of principled, purposeful leadership, a company will limp along in a continual state of dis-ease. In comparison to other businesses I've worked with, this Chamber of Commerce organization wasn't terribly malicious. People actually did come to work and feel OK. However, in order to sustain these good feelings, they had to compromise their instinctive sense of what a well-ordered company with clear direction and purpose looked like.

Just like a dysfunctional family, the dysfunctional business tries to pretend, as long as it can, that everything is just fine. This game of internal deception can go on almost forever. However, in this example, the real world of profit and loss eventually revealed the fact that "the Emperor had no clothes." In this case, their "nakedness" was brought to light in the form of constant complaints by members of their ethnic community, which saw that services were fragmented and attention to customer needs was inconsistent. If it weren't for the "push-back" on

You judge a person

like you judge an apple tree,

by the fruit it produces.

~ Abraham Maslow

the part of ill served clients, this business enterprise would have happily gone on its merry, dysfunctional way through my lifetime!

The second kind of dysfunction is derived from a personal experience: For a short time, I was one of the managers at a fitness resort for the "well heeled." While negotiating for the position, the resort's owner agreed to pay me a certain salary. Nothing, however, was in writing. On the first morning of the first day on the job, I went to say hello to my new boss. He was happily ensconced in a hot tub in the men's spa. After some preliminary greetings and inquiries about my relocation, he informed me that he couldn't possibly pay the salary that was quoted—that the sum was more than one of his other managers made, and he had been with the company for more than a year. There was little I could do to change his mind. That incident produced a smell of rotten fish; I felt I had made a big mistake not getting my salary offer in writing.

I soon discovered that my boss had a reputation for being "out of integrity." His dis-ease was that he couldn't be trusted. He had a habit of playing favorites. However, owing to his dis-ease the list of favorites would change from month to month. Operating in this setting was like being in "Alice in Wonderland." Reality changed from moment to moment. The place seemed like "1984" with a sauna! As you can well imagine, trying to manage in this kind of environment was next to impossible.

One never knew whether any of one's actions would be countermanded. Over time, the owner's dis-ease had become contagious throughout the resort. As a result, morale was always in the cellar, and people were quite secretive about their feelings. Not surprisingly, turnover was palpable and in-fighting was rampant.

Here we see an example of how a lack of integrity on the part of an owner/director created a deep sense of uncertainty and mistrust

Fear always springs from ignorance.

~ Ralph Waldo Emerson

throughout the organization. The higher the level of the source of dysfunction, the more it corrupts and contaminates the operation as a whole. This fellow's actions basically caused people to feel uncertain about how to effectively carry out their duties and responsibilities. This uncertainty eventually led to duplicity. People would "invent" things that they thought the boss wanted to hear, in order to avoid potential admonishment. It didn't matter whether you were a good worker or not. In fact, in such an environment of fear and paranoia, the worst performers often came out ahead, merely because they had a greater ability to deceive than their hard working counter-parts.

Let's talk about paranoia for a moment. Paranoia is a condition characterized by excessive fear and mistrust of others. In psychological terms, expressions of paranoia are considered unjustified. However, as I've seen countless times, paranoia in the workplace is often a normal response to the inherent dis-ease conditions within the work environment. In the presence of irrational and arbitrary authority, being paranoid becomes the only "healthy" way to survive.

Paranoia impairs one's ability to properly recognize dis-ease. People in paranoid work places attempt to adjust to abnormal conditions. After a while, life in "crazy" or "oppressive" businesses becomes merely "the way things work around here." This axiom is just as valid in troubled families as in places of business. Much like working under an unpredictable boss can seem normal, the abusive behavior of an alcoholic parent also seems normal, when viewed from the perspective of another member of that household.

In that sense businesses function much like family units. Elements of sickness can remain totally hidden from the outside world. Both extended family members and shareholders alike can be completely unaware of the dis-eases that dwell within.

Problems cannot be solved at the same level of awareness that created them.

~ Albert Einstein

Mistrust and the Game of Survival

From a systems perspective, mistrust is the deadliest dis-ease element, regardless of the type of institution under investigation. A lack of trust sucks the life blood out of a business. In the face of uncertainty, every thought and action becomes either reactive or defensive. The only strategy that is in play is the strategy of individual survival. Gradually, as skepticism rises, the infrastructure of the organization begins to weaken. At this juncture, people either abandon ship or become numb to the toxic nature of the environment itself.

In the shadow of mistrust lies fear. And in the presence of fear, creativity and forward movement are halted. This is why the nature of this form of dis-ease is so oppressive. The presence of mistrust means that everything is suspect. No solid ground exists to form healthy working relationships. Motives and intentions are scrutinized for hidden meanings that might spell harm to individuals or groups. All spontaneity and flexibility is lost. For the innocent people caught up in such situations, life can be very stressful. The only ones that benefit are those that thrive on chaos and disruption. Companies where low levels of trust exist are wretched places to work. Wheeling and dealing are the operative norms. In such environments everyone thinks themselves vulnerable. In the process, the purpose of the business is only a secondary consideration, at best.

Mistrust can arise as a result of any number of factors: repeated acts of dishonesty, lack of integrity, lack of fairness, favoritism, shifting loyalties, pursuit of personal agendas, preoccupation with power and control—the list of self-centered motives is almost endless.

Because mistrust as a dis-ease entity is so destructive, the strategies to eliminate it must be swift and decisive. Those responsible for spreading distrust must be held accountable. It often becomes difficult for

Whoever fights monsters

should see to it that in the process,

he does not become a monster.

~ Friedrich Nietzsche

perpetrators of mistrust to remain on board, so infectious is the dis-ease. If managers are part of the root causes for generating mistrust, and their actions are judged to be intentional, it might be impossible for the organization to regain its health and buoyancy without insisting on their departure.

A high degree of mistrust within a business inevitably gives rise to other insidious dis-eases, such as "turfism," power cliques, scape-goating, spreading "disinformation," undermining employee initiative and, in extreme cases, out and out sabotage.

If power within an organization is perceived to be corrupt, arbitrary or capricious, then the by-product will be mistrust, which, as we have seen, is the very foundation for dis-eases that may be so severe as to bring about the collapse of the business itself.

I experienced directly the effects of extreme mistrust with a former client. Late one evening I received a call from a plant manager of a firm that made computers—a firm, by the way, that is no longer in business. I had met this manager on a number of occasions at various community sponsored meetings. He was somewhat familiar with my work, having received several favorable comments from business associates about some of the projects I had undertaken.

He asked if I would meet him early the next morning at the plant, about "a matter of extreme urgency." I was presented with the following scenario: A day before I was contacted, a shipment of computers was delivered to a number of customers in several surrounding states. By late afternoon on the second day after shipment, calls started flooding the plant operator referencing the fact that the computers that were received in shipment weren't in operating condition.

The good man is the friend of

all living things.

~ Mahatma Gandhi

Further investigation revealed that when the main frame "boxes" were opened, assorted debris—everything from glue to motor oil—was discovered inside. Clearly someone had sabotaged the shipment. Eventually, I uncovered the fact that the production line was riddled with bitter and disgruntled workers, who deeply mistrusted several supervisors whom they regarded as discriminatory and harshly vindictive. Attempts to bring these matters to the attention of upper management proved fruitless. After a number of months of supposed ill treatment, the line employees erupted. This degree of corporate sabotage is rare. Nevertheless, it brings home the point with abundant clarity: *When people in positions of power become abusive to the point of engendering deep seated mistrust about their actions, some form of "push-back" is inevitable.*

Companies that have authoritarian management structures are primary breeding grounds for mistrust. In these environments employees feel they are under "tight control"—another way of saying that management doesn't trust them. Workers of all types crave meaningful involvement. They want the opportunity to contribute to the decision making process. They seek an opportunity to offer input about policies and procedures that directly effect them.

However, when these things are absent, a ticking time bomb is set off. Push-back responses are likely to occur when people are denied forms of expression that elevate their sense of being valued. Environments that engender suspicion—that lack basic integrity—undermine that sense of value that employees need to feel purposeful and fully engaged. In its final stages, as we have seen above, responses might escalate into subversive acts which are designed to demonstrate the high level of frustration and powerlessness that exists.

No one is useless in this world

who lightens the burdens of others.

~ Charles Dickens

The Value of Valuing

The act of "pushing back" is an expression not just of anger, but of an attempt to preserve one's sense of self esteem. I've seen many people walk away from oppressive work environments knowing full well that the task of finding another job would be difficult—all because they felt their jobs did not enhance their "pride of self." The need for self esteem is critical. When it is fully present in employees, it is a clear sign that the company feels vital and full of purpose.

I distinctly recall a discussion with a high placed executive in Silicon Valley, who, after praising me for my work with one of his subordinate groups, told me he was leaving the company to set up his own business. Knowing that he made a high six figure salary, I asked him what motivated him to go out on his own. His reply was somewhat disarming. "No one," he said, "has ever told me I've done a good job." He went on to talk about the fact that through all his years of service, and all his salary increases, no one seemed to recognize and honor his contribution to the company. Basically, the job did not, in any way, contribute to his sense of "self-worth." Because of this, he felt "worth-less," despite his hefty pay check.

If a business fails to contribute to the enhancement of an individual's self esteem, the business will, over time, create a dis-eased employee. To illustrate this point in some detail, allow me to share with you the story of a large, city-run, fleet management operation which seemed to be in the business of lowering self-esteem.

If you don't already know, fleet management operations are responsible for maintaining a company's vehicles. In the case of a city, the vehicles would include heavy mechanized operating equipment, garbage and repair trucks, and sometimes police cars. The fleet service

One of the keys to happiness

is a bad memory.

~ Rita Mae Brown

in question, was about to be privatized. Operations were near collapse. Chaos ruled the day.

When I arrived at the Fleet yards, I discovered that most vehicles that came in for major repairs were back in the shop in a week to ten days. There was no system in place for standard preventive maintenance. In addition, it was openly acknowledged that many of the city's cars were "dangerous to drive." The police force was so gun shy about sending their cars to Fleet, they did their own repairs and maintenance—placing yet another drain on the city's coffers. To make matters even worse, an out and out hatred existed between service crews and supervisors. It was not uncommon for supervisors' cars to be "trashed"—tires flattened, lights smashed, hoses slashed—so much so, that supervisory personnel would park blocks away from the Fleet parking lot to avoid being targeted.

On the shop floor, a gang-like mentality prevailed. Informal "leaders" could easily promote work slow downs or prompt nasty confrontations with line supervisors. On the line, supervisors were authoritarian and vengeful. If a supervisor disliked someone, he would assign that person a job which would normally require the work of at least two men. Adding to this nightmare, inventories records were all but non-existent, and theft was commonplace. (I later learned that a few of the line staff had businesses on the side selling the stolen inventory items.)

Here was an environment of raw, primitive survival where might was the clear winner over right, and power in whatever form, dictated what was done and what was not. The racial and ethnic composition was such that my Spanish speaking skills helped gain entry into the mechanic service clique, which was the operational core of discontent. After I was judged to be harmless and full of "strange" humor, I was allowed to spend time crawling under Cummins engines to

I don't know the key to success,

but the key to failure is trying

to please everybody.

~ Bing Crosby

listen to what people had to say. Eventually, I even worked my way into some local restaurants to get the first hand nitty-gritty about the nature of dis-ease at Fleet.

After an exhaustive operations assessment, one single truth emerged: no one in the Fleet service, short of the invisible executives that were on the top management tier, felt valued. On the contrary, the majority felt "worth-less." Virtually all of the acting out behavior on both sides of the worker-supervisor fence was a result of the mistrust that emerged from the "devaluation" of each person toward the other. Given this mess, where was I to begin? Obviously, the "dis-eased norms" that lowered self esteem had to be changed. Being "worth-less" had to metamorphose into being highly valued. Likewise, the deep mistrust which permeated every part of the operation needed to be excised.

I reasoned that in order to achieve these objectives, certain rock solid systems of accountability needed to be put in place: inventories had to be computerized, vehicles had to be assessed as to what was wrong, what was fixed, etc. When a car left the shop, we had to document who did the work. Fairness and accountability became the operative buzz words.

It was obvious that most of the assessment information could be turned into data and entered into a computer utilizing a special program. Not much rocket science there. But what was special was the notion of forming self-selected work teams and, in the process, restructure the duties of each line supervisor.

This was risky business. But, as Bob Dylan said in one of his songs, "When you ain't got nothin', you got nothin' to lose." I managed to convince upper management to go along with the plan. At first, they were horrified. They felt that all the bullies and "gangsters" would group into one team, leading to a complete reign of terror. I tried to

Some changes are so slow

you don't notice them.

Others are so fast

they don't notice you.

~ Ashleigh Brilliant

reduce their fear level by explaining that in the new configuration it would be the teams themselves that would determine who would do the work and how it would be accomplished. Under the new arrangement, supervisors would be responsible for supplying the team with the parts they needed, entering data on the nature of the repairs, and negotiating with the team about the volume of work that should be done each day.

As incentive, I established that after a trial period of sixty days, if all vehicles leaving Fleet were judged to be in good working order, then, upon completion of each day's assignments, each team could leave work up to a half hour earlier than their usual clock-out time. After all, what we were interested in was high quality performance and productivity. If all that could be achieved in less than the usual work day, so much the better for all concerned.

Before the program could officially get underway, we had to first conduct some unpleasant but necessary business. Several of the most malevolent employees had to go. There was no saving these guys. They were toxic to the operation. Nothing would change that. Each of the employees that were to be "termed" had long histories of disruption and inappropriate behavior. Yet, the managers at Fleet were reluctant to engage in this action, fearing reprisals from the other mechanics. Finally, after much urging, the bosses bit their lips and "cut bait."

Ironically, very little was said once the dismissals took place, save to comment that these measures should have been implemented long ago. Because of this action, and, in view of the changes that were taking place, management was beginning to gather back a little of the credibility that had been absent for a long time.

It's important that management should never underestimate the sophistication of the front line worker. For the most part, they are keenly

If you can find a path with no obstacles,

it probably leads to nowhere.

~ Anonymous

aware of what's going on. They have a "gut" understanding of what is intrinsically fair and unfair. The mechanics at Fleet were well aware of the co-workers who were helping to paralyze the operation. They had lost respect in management for keeping many of these guys on the job. However, none would ever admit to it. The very act of keeping destructive employees on board is doubly harmful, in that management, by failing to take appropriate action, engenders nothing but contempt, disrespect and mistrust throughout the lower ranks.

True to the managers' worst fears, the bullies and "gangsters" did join the same teams. But this time, things were different. Instead of attempting to undermine operations, they did everything they could to make their team the top performers. They simply could not accept being second best. Consequently, peer pressure to perform was the most intense in the "gangster team." (I can remember seeing them sneer with delight whenever they got to leave work a half hour earlier than their co-workers.) A minor miracle was unfolding right before my eyes. Eventually, the police, who were impressed by the marked turn around, ceased their own repair and maintenance work, and transferred all service operations back to Fleet. Now THAT was real victory!

Truth be told, things did not always run smoothly in this transitional turn around. Some team member changes were needed in the starting weeks of the program. Several supervisors had to be reassigned. Negotiations as to what constituted a "fair day's work" had to be hashed and rehashed. But, in retrospect, this was all "process." Essentially, the program gave value to everyone and emphasized the importance of quality and accountability. The added incentives acted to keep the motivation high.

Obviously, one of the big challenges was making these arbitrary groups of mechanics into real team players—dividing work loads, making proper decisions, sharing skills and technical knowledge,

Nothing is as it seems,

but everything is exactly like it is.

~ Yogi Berra

settling disagreements, developing consistent internal performance standards, etc. Yet, when given the opportunity to have a say in how work was accomplished, almost everyone, to the man, rose to the occasion. Even in the early days of trying things out, there was present a certain enthusiasm and motivation that was completely lacking in their previous work environment.

I was particularly impressed by the willingness of those mechanics to share their knowledge and skills by becoming mentors and coaches to their peers—some of whom were on "rival" teams. In their former work lives, individual survival was the name of the game.

Also, in their former toxic work setting, possessing certain skills was a coveted strategic advantage. It was used as device to control weaker, less skilled co-workers and supervisors. It's evident, in this brief case study, how mistrust and devaluation can degenerate into organized chaos. However, this was an extreme example, with extreme consequences. I could have just as easily described milder forms of dysfunction which, over the long term, erode self esteem: hard working secretaries whose bosses never say "good job;" middle managers who spend countless hours making sure everything is running well, never to receive even a hint of a "thank you;" computer programmers who always offer a helping hand to anyone running into problems, but never receive any recognition or reward for their acts of selfless generosity. After a while, it's only natural for employees to ask themselves, "What's missing here?" "Why do I feel so empty when I come into work?" "Doesn't anyone appreciate who I am, or what I'm doing?" When employees begin asking these kinds of questions, the seeds of dis-ease have already been firmly planted.

Employees, in fact, don't need authoritarian work places to be suspect of their company or the way they are managed. Mistrust can be a subtle emotion. It can arise incrementally, over time. Actions by man-

Self-esteem is the reputation we acquire

with ourselves.

~ Nathaniel Branden

agement which produce a lack of confidence in the decision making process, will start to generate these types of feelings. Even small shifts in attitude can bring about changes in performance and productivity.

The Challenge of Proper Rewards and Recognition

There is a direct correlation between the way a company values its employees and the degree of excellence those employees exhibit in producing goods and delivering services. Clearly, not enough emphasis is placed on developing the kinds of rewards or recognition which propel individuals to greater levels of achievement.

Many so-called "Reward & Recognition Programs" are not well thought out. Rewards and recognition need to be linked to easily understood performance goals. Managers must be fair and unbiased in determining who deserves to be recognized. It's always a good idea for employees to be able to reward their peers. There should never be just one form of reward. Small, non-monetary gifts, award certificates, impromptu recognitions, fun activities—the list of ways to reward and liven up a work setting is limited only to the imagination. However, if handled incorrectly, rewards programs can do more harm than good.

I once consulted for a business where the internal "vibes" were so awful, and the atmosphere so polluted with mistrust, that only a handful of the company's 800 employees ever showed up at the company's annual picnic. The managers thought this had to do with the fact that the place was full of unappreciative employees, who "didn't deserve a picnic to begin with." Actually, their poor attendance was more a reflection of working for a company that de-valued people at every opportunity—save for the company picnic. The exceptionally poor turn out was adequate testimony to what wasn't happening the other 364 days of the year!

The point we emphasize is strong confidence

in our original nature.

~ Shunryu Suzuki

The issue of how employees are valued becomes central to the quest for performance excellence. Programs which reward and recognize can't be a last minute afterthought, nor should they be included only "if there's money in the budget." It must be treated as a "hand and glove" function, running parallel with high performance standards and equitable management practices.

It makes sense for employers to spend time carefully considering the nature of value in the workplace. The desire to feel valued in one's job has become a necessary component to a positive outlook about one's position in the society at large. This fundamental need applies equally to a top executive or the fellow who sweeps the floor at night when everyone goes home.

Feeling valued in a business indicates that you mean something to the organization; that the work you do is considered important and vital to the success of the entire operation. In the Fleet Management case study that was cited, workers were treated as "paid slave labor." No one was ever consulted about how work should be performed. Personal views were considered irrelevant or, as the mechanics put it, "not worth squat." Further, because they were managed authoritatively, they reacted by being angry and mistrustful. Before too long, these feelings turned into a full blown dis-ease, and open rebellion ensued.

Psychologists are quick to point out that people, especially those in western cultures have strong ego needs. This means that it's important for them to be recognized as distinct individuals—not as ants in a vast undifferentiated colony. If the person is deprived of basic ego need requirements, chances are good they will become alienated and bitter. People like this—and there are lots of them in North America, tend to develop feelings of isolation as an initial response to this condition. This makes coming together to share ideas an uphill battle. In severely dis-eased settings, such as the Fleet operation or the comput-

The trouble with the rat race is that

even if you win, you're still a rat.

~ Lily Tomlin

er manufacturing plant that was referenced earlier, alienation quickly gave way to frustration and anger. Even in less extreme cases, loss of essential ego sustaining requirements drain both physical and psychic energy, making performances less focused and error prone.

Environments such as these sap the energy from any individual who feels inspired to think or do anything other than his or her mundane assignments. If, as is sometimes the case, a new management philosophy is put in place, with new people in charge, the positive effects are often not felt for many months. Mistrust and alienation cannot be cured overnight. Just as people are traumatized by combat experiences, there is a similar "post-traumatic-stress-syndrome" that effects employees that have worked under demeaning management. It takes much good will, patience, and subtle encouragement to start bringing traumatized employees back to life.

Once, while traveling in Greece as a graduate student, I took a boat to an island called Tenos. Not much was said about it in the guidebooks, however, I thought it might be worth visiting. As soon as I stepped off the dock, I was astounded to discover that almost everyone there was crippled. I wanted to leave immediately, but it was too late. My boat had already left for another island. It would be three days until another would arrive.

Tenos, it seems, is the site of a church which contains the sacred relic of a saint. Once a year, every crippled person from surrounding islands ventures to Tenos to pray to the relic to be healed. By the afternoon of the second day, I found it difficult to walk upright; I think I even started to limp after the first day. Since that time, whenever I see a business that does not allow employees to feel valued, I think of Tenos and those poor cripples. It's tough to work in places where the majority of workers feel disabled. Yet, thousands of people, some in suits, others in coveralls, do just that day after day.

Is the system going to flatten you out

and deny you your humanity, or are

you going to be able to make use of

the system to the attainment of

human purposes ?

~ Joseph Campbell

The Dis-ease of Disconnection

If we step back a bit, we notice that the same dis-ease characteristics—mistrust, lack of integrity, poor management of subordinates, and a lowering of self esteem—are also dis-ease characteristics for many kinds of institutions other than for-profit businesses. Take, for example, the area of public education. I once facilitated a workshop that brought together professors of educational administration and public school principals for the purpose of discussing ways in which the education and training of public school administrators could be made more relevant to life "in the field." Before too long, the temperament of the discussions turned sour. The meeting bore a striking resemblance to groups of contentious managers and employees I had worked with in the past. The administration professors, many of whom taught the principals that were in attendance, seemed defensive and even self-righteous about the "correctness" of their approach toward educating administrators.

The principals appeared be to even more frustrated than the professors. They didn't appreciate what seemed to be close-minded attitudes and values. They felt the professors didn't know much about what it was actually like to be a principal in a public school.

Unfortunately, this three day workshop concluded with a heavy amount of resentment on both sides. The principals, especially, seemed discouraged by the experience of coming together with people who were responsible for preparing individuals to administrate local schools who had little sympathy or understanding for their plight. It was obvious that the principals wanted to feel supported in their efforts to educate the children in their communities, in the face of incredibly limited resources.

They wanted these education professors to say something that would provide, if not hope, then encouragement, that their challenges were

Don't listen to what they say. Go see.

~ Chinese Proverb

not merely crosses to be borne in stoic silence. This didn't happen. The principals returned to their schools feeling helpless and unsupported by the very people who claimed to have a handle on what public education was supposed to look like.

The dynamics of these two "inter-locking" groups of educators paralleled, to an uncanny degree, many aspects of dis-eased companies. The university administrators functioned much like managers, the principals, like employees. After a short time together, feelings of mistrust arose from both sides. Neither group was really listening to the other. Each party wanted to demonstrate the correctness of their approach to education. The principals left feeling discouraged, just as many workers feel when there is a loss of a collective "spirit" of intention and purpose. The education professors were offended, because their lofty positions as authority figures had been put into question. It was a Mexican Standoff. Nothing was accomplished.

What we see emerging in the examples cited, is a complex pattern of dis-ease that can overtake any group of managers and employees. Somewhere along the line, the business loses its sense of direction and purpose. Without a clarity of purpose, the enterprise starts to slowly come apart.

What is most evident about this type of fragmentation is the failure of both employees and managers to ask fundamental questions about the nature of the enterprise itself. *It's truly amazing how many organizational entities can operate year after year without really addressing core questions that have to do with products, services and the interface of people.*

Over time, when everyone is feeling uneasy because no one is asking the important questions, even rhetorically, the operation itself merely "play acts" at doing its job and performing its functions. There's no juice. There's no life. There's no energized spirit. This is the stage

Fortune favors the audacious.

~ Desiderius Erasmus

where many employees feel that they are doing nothing more than "collecting a paycheck."

The Dis-ease of Discouragement

For many individuals caught up in such scenarios, particularly those who are concerned about "making a difference," a feeling of discouragement overtakes their day-to-day work life, destroying confidence and sapping energy. Discouragement represents a loss of courage. Allow me to provide a graphic example: On a visit to Thailand, I decided to take a trip to the countryside, just outside of Bangkok. I wanted to see how they trained work elephants. Little did I know what lessons I would learn on that hot, humid afternoon.

The Thai's have developed a fool proof method for completely destroying confidence and willpower when they tame elephants. As babies, the elephants have their legs chained and tied to heavy wooden rods that are driven in the ground. Because of this bondage, their movements are greatly restricted. Try as they might, they can't break free of their chains.

After many months of being shackled in this manner, the thickness of the chain, and how deeply it's buried, no longer matters. The huge animal can be restrained by merely tying a thin rope around one leg attached to a small peg which is then tapped into the earth. Because of repressive conditioning, the huge beast no longer has a will to move or break free. In other words, the elephant has become, "discouraged"—he has lost his courage to be spontaneous and carefree in his movements.

The dictionary defines courage as, "the state or quality of mind or spirit that enables one to face danger, fear, or vicissitudes with self pos-

There are costs and risks

to a program of action,

but they are far less than the long range

risks and costs of inaction.

~ John F. Kennedy

session, confidence, resolution and bravery." Given the challenges that exist in today's business world, courage seems to be exactly what's called for. However, workplace dysfunction produces just the opposite effect. People in dis-eased environments try to develop personal tactics for staying safe, in a milieu riddled with uncertainty. Courage implies a willingness to deal with threats and uncertainties, but this response is one that few are willing to take. Far better to join a "turf clique" and be shielded from outside danger, or try to remain anonymous and passive, than to face the threat of termination. These and similar tactics are the result of the politics of discouragement. They exist in both subtle and extreme dimensions. In whatever form it appears, discouragement erodes positive energy and retards growth and flexibility. At the very least, a discouraged work force can never rise above mediocrity. Once clear objectives, empowerment and a fair system of incentive and accountability are nurtured and put into place, the seeds that breed discouragement dry up and lose their potency. As confidence rises, the hold that discouragement has on employees is lifted.

Courage plays a particularly important role in the behaviors of managers. Given our current unstable markets, nervous investors and suspicion about the security of one's retirement, courageous management performing in the face of uncertainty will gain the confidence and loyalty of apprehensive employees.

But to achieve this state of employee confidence, companies must be dissuaded from thinking only about short term gains and losses. They, too, must act courageously in seeking solutions to their obstinate internal dis-eases. They, too must be willing to take calculated risks to build high performance businesses where fear and discouragement are not in such toxic abundance.

Looking once again at the Fleet management case, we find ample evidence to support the claim that various forms of recognition, empow-

If you refuse to accept anything but the best

out of life, you very often get it.

~ Somerset Maugham

erment and incentives converted this sluggish, impaired operation into one filled with courageous performers who willingly collaborated to produce positive outcomes. In Fleet's case, the primary change agent was shared decision making. That process did not come easily. After the initial anger and hostility dissipated, what remained were people who knew only how to respond negatively. In appearance and action, they were much like those chained elephants in Thailand or the quadriplegics in Greece—discouraged and disabled.

Their dis-eased condition fostered so much animosity and mistrust that, as an organization, they could no longer solve problems on their own. When operations degenerate to the degree that this Fleet service did, great objectivity is needed to develop strategies for repair and renewal.

There is widespread belief that dysfunctional elements within a company can be fixed much like a tire that goes flat. Boom! The tire blows out. What now? Just call road service and you'll be up and running in no time. Right? Not hardly! When companies become places that harbor mistrust, dishonesty, questionable integrity and overtly authoritative management, they require specialists who can step back and look objectively at the enterprise.

Regrettably, most human resource departments are ill equipped to be given these kinds of assignments. They are, themselves, too caught up in the malaise—not to mention that often they have played a role in fostering the dis-ease process itself. At times, their motives and intentions are linked with those of upper management. And after all, wasn't it upper management's "ignor-ance" of degenerating conditions that allowed the situation to become toxic? One might question the inherent logic of this kind of thinking. However, dis-eased organizations are, by definition, ones that can't think or act with sustained clarity.

We are what we think:

All that we are arises with our thoughts.

With our thoughts we make the world.

~ Shakyamuni Buddha

Trying to empower formerly disempowered employees without a master plan is courting disaster. In Fleet's case, once the mechanics were given decision-making responsibilities, they had no idea what to do. (Some men at Fleet even commented that in the early stages of the change initiative, they felt so uncertain about how to proceed, they wished they were back operating under the old tyrannical regime. At least in that setting, they knew how to behave.)

Discouraged workers must be encouraged, guided and persuaded to look at old habits and attitudes with new eyes. They must be assured, that within reasonable limits, mistakes are permitted. Malcolm Forbes once said "failure is success if we learn from it." Moving away from dis-ease patterns involves both learning and re-learning. Damaged businesses will not recover on the basis of their "know-how," but only through their "learn how."

This means being proactive when looking at operations that aren't working right. It also means asking rudimentary questions, such as, "What are we all about, as a business?" or "How can we avoid the mistakes we just made the next time around?" The personnel at Fleet had to learn from scratch how to talk to one another. They needed to reexamine, as a group, what repair work was all about. When they did, they discovered that Joe had a better way to fix a broken axle, or that Pete could be working more efficiently if he thought out the repair procedure before getting started.

Gradually, as these men became comfortable with thinking about the "bigger picture" they found there were ways to do things that could save both time and money. And even more to the point, they were encouraged to do just that. When they did, the perception they had of themselves and their job also changed—much to the better!

It is easier to fight for one's principles

than it is to live up to them.

~ Alfred Adler

Discussing how things should operate was hard at first. Initially, the collective "huddles" that were put in place had to be facilitated. But once the teams realized that they weren't being judged or disciplined for their actions, they started to lighten up. That's when real progress happened. In a short while, the teams were voluntarily sharing what they learned with one another. Competition was now turned into collective striving.

The Bain of the Band-Aid Fix

The changes that took place in Fleet exemplify that even in the presence of marked distrust and overt hostility, work settings can be converted into places where healthy competition is the norm. One thing that is both disheartening and irksome is to see a poorly functioning operation continue to deteriorate (sometimes rapidly) because of management's refusal to take the bull by the horns and admit that things are "screwed up." "Denial," as the saying goes, "is more than just a river in Egypt."

Denial, which is a refusal to recognize or admit that there is something very wrong with the business operation, is a fundamental characteristic of a dysfunctional business. Many of my experiences of organizational denial come from various service industries, such as hotels, resorts and high end gaming establishments, but are also present in great numbers in both government and non-profit environments. Hotels, in particular, struck me as being masters of the "quick fix." Their approach to solving internal problems is strongly influenced by their tendency to offer low wages, provide little substantive training and demand high performance, all at the same time. It's not just a coincidence that turnover in this industry is off the charts.

Beyond living and dreaming

there is something more important:

Waking up.

~ Antonio Machado

Sadly, by maintaining these kinds of practices, the hospitality industry in particular acts to devalue the importance of growing people within their organization, despite wide claims to the contrary. This is true at both the line level and in various supervisory and management positions. Relative to other industries, service industries, including restaurants and many small business enterprises which rely on the influx of cheap labor, are flagrantly "dis-couraging."

I recall explaining to one general manager at a luxury hotel, which was part of a huge national chain, the many dysfunctional areas within the organization that needed to change. When I finished my analysis, he looked a bit perplexed, and muttered, "You mean you can't take care of this in a weekend workshop?" The funny thing is, he was dead serious!

It's a disappointing fact that when businesses finally reach the stage where they feel something MUST be done, things have usually degenerated to the degree that a major "sea-change" is required. At that juncture, there is often a reluctance to engage in the kind of in-depth work necessary to cure the ills that are setting the business on a steep declining curve. Instead, many companies opt for the "band-aid cure" which is basically a superficial attempt to gloss over what is really going on.

I've become convinced that the so-called band-aid cure is sometimes applied because of an innate fear that once a thorough investigation of the organization's dis-eases gets underway, the finger will point upward to levels of management that would rather remain beyond reproach. In other words, putting band-aids on "running organizational sores" is often a defensive measure used to deflect responsibility downward into the lower ranks.

I have had many occasions to witness band-aid approaches in the hospitality industry. One that was especially noteworthy took place

For every expert,

there is an equal and opposite expert.

~ Arthur C. Clarke

at a luxury hotel which catered primarily to business travelers. Like many other hotels I've assisted, this one did not seriously attempt to correct operational shortcomings. For example, staff turnover was a nagging issue which was virtually ignored. As one might imagine, because this issue was ignored, guest service was always marginal.

My initial evaluation indicated that the factors which contributed to this excessive turnover were directly related to piecemeal training, low wages and authoritarian control. I wondered why everyone missed this connection. After all, how can you possibly expect people to deliver superior guest service, and handle all the behind-the-scenes responsibilities while failing to provide the necessary service training, along with acceptable wages? Is it any wonder that personnel came and went like shoppers through a department store close-out sale?

One of the factors that contributed to the collective managerial "ignorance" of this establishment was the rigid operating budget that was imposed upon the hotel by their regional corporate bosses. General managers had little say in determining the scope of the budget. In fact, to be overly vocal about the "numbers" put one's job at risk. People were expected to constantly do more with less. But God-forbid if you succeeded in operating within this budget. If you did, during the next budget cycle, you would be asked to do even more with even less.

Over a long period of time, I've observed a rather interesting characteristic in large organizations, namely, *the higher up you go in an outfit, particularly in the corporate sphere, the more you talk "numbers" and the less you talk "people."* The tacit message that often is transmitted from the corporate office to the field is "just do it"—no matter how much dis-couragement and bloodletting ensues.

At one leading casino company, my client had developed a system of linking customer satisfaction with offering employee bonuses.

Reality is merely an illusion,

albeit a very persistent one.

~ Albert Einstein

However, the system was grossly flawed. I saw this first hand at many of their facilities. Managers admitted in hushed tones that they knew the system was defective, however they also knew that to deliver that message to the company's COO would be equivalent to signing your own death warrant. Anyone with any savvy knew that the people at the top had no qualms about shooting the messenger. As a result, people instinctively kept their mouths tightly shut.

Eventually, the survey of guest responses was revamped. Somehow, the negativity surrounding this evaluative format finally managed to "ooze" its way up the ladder, inside to the corporate offices. It's truly remarkable how out of touch "corporate" can be with field offices. They often seem to operate with two distinctly different sets of values and objectives.

Certainly this was the case with the business hotel cited earlier. The general manager there continued to "play dumb" and support the tyranny of the corporate office. In response to my question about inadequate training, he became somewhat defensive, telling me that every new employee is assigned a "mentor" to cover all work responsibilities during the first week on the job. I decided to find out how effective this mentoring business was.

The front desk appeared to be a good place to start. Anyone who knows anything about hotels is aware that the front desk is the communication nerve center of the entire operation. I learned that because of short staffing—which was put into effect as a cost cutting measure—"mentors" were constantly slammed with a hundred and one tasks. This left little or no time to help out the novices. The novices, in turn, were quite inept at handling just about anything: They fumbled with the computer registration program, were clueless in their handling of guest complaints and had a poor professional presence.

We can never have enough of that

which we really do not want.

~ Eric Hoffer

They also had real trouble getting their priorities straight: Do they answer a phone call first, and leave a guest waiting for service? Watching these antics from afar was like viewing a scene from a Marx Brothers' film. Yet, truth be told, this was far from a laughing matter. Compounding the scenario was the fact that these poor, stressed out souls at the front desk didn't have the time or the skills to think about proper etiquette in their interface with both guests and co-workers.

After more professional snooping, I uncovered other facts. For example, most of the maintenance people found the front desk folk so abrupt and discourteous that they simply turned their radios off so they wouldn't have to "put up with all their crap." This rebellious gesture caused further delays in responding to guest requests. (One of which involved a broken toilet gushing water into an elderly guest's bathroom!)

Obviously, the groping inefficiency at the hotel's information center was duly noted by even the most passive guests. In order to try to stave off the more aggressive business patrons, who vehemently demanded decent service, the front desk manager performed another "band aid job" by hiring yet another untrained front desk clerk. This one happened to be an attractive young woman. When faced with situations or tasks she didn't understand, she would look forlorn, blink her bright blue eyes and giggle innocently. Most of the middle-aged manager types standing in the check-in line would melt in polite acceptance.

However, this benign tolerance came to a grinding halt every weekend when the businessmen were replaced by stressed out, vacationing families with screaming kids. When I paid a return visit to the hotel a short time later, I wasn't surprised to find that the lovely damsel in question had been replaced. The law of the jungle once again reared its ugly head! Perhaps a bit of proper training might have saved the

Every individual is an expression of the whole realm of nature, a unique action of the total universe.

~ Alan Watts

day—and saved the added expense of finding yet another unskilled replacement! But problems at the front desk were far from over.

Aside from garnering the disrespect of the boys in maintenance, the front desk personnel were also snubbed by the hotel's sales reps. They viewed these young innocents as hapless duds, not worthy of attention. However, in interlocking service organizations, like this one, mutual support is THE one and only formula for success.

Given the range of negativity that existed from one service area to another, this level of support was nothing but a pipe dream. When the sales department needed any information from the front desk they found them uncooperative and resistant. The exception to this pattern was one sales rep who seemed to be a happy camper.

She always got what she wanted in a timely fashion. When I interviewed her she told me that the problem with her sales rep colleagues was that they didn't take the time to get to know any of the front desk clerks.

She went on to explain:

When someone new comes to work at the front desk, I make it a point to go up and introduce myself. I tell them who I am, what I do, and ask them where they're from and how they came to work for the hotel. Then, I try to take them to lunch or coffee or something. From that time on, anything I need, I get. It doesn't matter if I'm in a hurry, I always manage to say, "hi." It pays to make friends with the front desk people. They can save you a lot of time and hassle. Anyway..., I like people, that's why I do what I do.

These candid remarks contain a wealth of information. So many operational difficulties can be overcome through the act of building positive relationships. Why this simple axiom eludes so many managers in all types of businesses remains a mystery. The building of social relation-

Originality and the feeling

of one's own dignity are achieved

only through work and struggle.

~ Fyodor Dostoyevsky

ships serves many vital functions. First and foremost, it establishes familiarity. Making contact with someone gives them a human face, and along with that face comes an association. If that association is positive, then the probability for equally positive dialogue expands exponentially.

Similarly, actively building positive relationships breaks down artificial barriers, such as those imposed by title, rank or connection with other groups or individuals. Getting to know someone by more than just name and title clarifies perceptions that one person might develop for the other. Further, building relationships promotes empathy. It allows the other person to understand a bit more what your role in the organization is and what kind of challenges and obstacles you face from day to day.

It's so helpful for a business, particularly one with a diverse array of job functions, to have a staff that has a good feel for what it's like to be in the shoes of their co-workers. As such, I strongly advocate training programs which allow people to develop more than just a superficial understanding of other people's duties. In essence, it's another more sophisticated form of relationship building.

Communication Breakdowns

In the program that was developed for this hotel, I designed a new employee orientation which placed people in different job settings for two half days. The end result was notable. Formerly hostile departments now had a keen awareness of how difficult it was to perform other tasks. Sales reps, for example, developed a new-found respect for people in food and beverage. Likewise, front desk clerks got a real "feel" for how difficult it was to be an engineer. After their exposure to the daily life in hotel maintenance, these clerks were far less likely to bark orders at people over the radio. Building relation-

Our opinion of people depends less upon

what we see in them than upon what

they make us see in ourselves.

~ Sarah Grand

ships through exposure to other jobs within the company has the effect of aligning people in the belief that the operation is a complex interactive organism, where one part contributes to the success (or failure) of the other.

Likewise, for managers to become effective leaders, building relationships allows for a more candid way to discover how your peers and subordinates "see the world." Knowing what people are thinking and how they perceive challenges and events—particularly those that involve change initiatives—become invaluable tools for leading people.

Effective leaders are people who shape and influence opinions and actions for the purpose of producing specific results. There is no better way to do this than to construct a network of social relationships throughout the operation. This should become a standard practice for anyone in management.

I'm often called upon to conduct assessments of businesses to ascertain what is politely known as "areas of opportunity," (eg., "Where are we screwed up?") I make a point to spend time building friendly relationships. For a consultant, credibility and trust comes first!

After a relatively short period, I'm able to put together a detailed profile of what these "areas of opportunity" look like. Many times I have to chuckle to myself when I see the startled faces of top execs following a preliminary briefing prior to submission of my official report. They just can't fathom how I managed to learn so much in a week or two.

Once again, it's all about relationships. Good relationship building allows trust and credibility to emerge more spontaneously. It becomes the starting point from which supportive followers emerge. As we have seen, non-managers also greatly benefit from relationship building, as our hotel sales rep demonstrated.

Too much of a good thing

can be wonderful.

~ Mae West

However, her understanding of the importance of building relationships outside her own sales department was not shared by the majority of her colleagues. When it comes to the "art" of building positive relationships, if you don't have it, you must learn it. North American companies are relatively backward in the value they place on formally engaging in meaningful encounters. They need books like *The One Minute Manager* to tell them that it makes sense to walk around and talk to people.

By contrast, non-western cultures seem to have a built-in understanding that fostering harmonious relationships in one's place of work helps create "on-purpose" work forces. For example, the Japanese have a concept called *Ningen Kankei,* which translates roughly as "social relationships." In Japanese business the application of *Ningen Kankei* acts to support the group in establishing social harmony.

The noted anthropologist Edward T. Hall refers to Japan as a "high context" society—one where information is expected to be shared with everyone. If you were to go to a corporate headquarters in Japan and peer into the executive offices, chances are you'd find everyone housed in the same room. This is because, in Japan, it's everyone's responsibility to share information. It strikes the Japanese as very bizarre that here in America, we place executives and managers in their own offices. Because of this "isolation" countless problems arise. We, in North America, just can't seem to draw the proper link between relationship building and effective management. When it does happen, it is more a result of individual managers "doing their thing," rather than a formal strategy for creating real consensus within the organization.

Returning to our hotel example, I uncovered further instances of how ignoring social relationships undermined operations. Venturing into the housekeeping department, I learned that most of the housekeep-

Today, we know that all

human beings who strive to maintain

life and who long to be spared pain,

all living beings on earth

are our neighbors.

~ Albert Schweitzer

ers were Spanish-speaking "Latinas." By contrast, the rest of the hotel were primarily English-speaking Caucasians. The Executive Housekeeper, another Caucasian, could speak only a few words of Spanish. Right away, I knew this language gap between director and staff would lead to trouble. I was right.

The hotel, it seems, did not have any program in place which recognized the existence of diverse racial and ethnic groups. Recognizing diversity within a company acts as a form of team building. To overlook the presence of distinct racial or ethnic groups within a work force is to insure fragmentation and increase the probability that disease will arise.

The hotel in question was no exception. Not a single non-Latino took the time to learn even one word of Spanish. Few, if any, staff members called any housekeeper by name, even though name tags were prominently displayed on each uniform. The majority of housekeepers seemed to be shy and retiring—they felt alienated and insecure because they were held "at arms length" by rest of the hotel's employees. Consciously or not, this property had transformed these diligent, hard working people into second class citizens.

Every day they could be seen bringing food to the housekeeping office, avoiding the employee cafeteria altogether. The Engineering Department, in particular, kept the housekeepers at a distance. What bothered them was their discontent with having to constantly repair broken electric plugs on vacuum cleaners. This situation occurred because the housekeepers had developed the bad habit of yanking cords out of their electrical sockets rather than gently unplugging them. However, no one would ever make the effort to bring this matter to their attention. In order to send out a message that he was upset about having to divert his crew from larger projects to fix these machines, the Chief Engineer would delay necessary repair

Sometimes I think God, in creating man,

somewhat overestimated his ability.

~ Oscar Wilde

work. This, in turn, led to a shortage of working vacuum cleaners. Housekeepers were now forced to share equipment with one another, which then resulted in internal squabbling. Given all the ensuing confusion, there were rooms that didn't get properly cleaned. The Executive Housekeeper, after living with this situation for months, developed a nasty grudge against her engineering colleagues and refused to help that department if the need arose.

In the following months, before I came on board, these Directors had no personal contact. Instead, they sent out sharp, critical memos through the email—even though their offices were only twenty feet apart. Adding to these complications was the fact that the Assistant Executive Housekeeper, who was herself Spanish speaking, had applied for the job of Executive Housekeeper. Instead, it was given to an outside applicant, which was now her boss. (Her subordinates referred to her as "La Gringa"—a negative term for a non-Latino from North America.)

As situations unfolded, the Assistant Executive Housekeeper resented the fact that her boss made no effort to bridge the language gap. This, she felt, placed an additional burden on her. Apart from other duties, she now had to serve as her boss' personal translator. This was perceived as a particularly irksome task and resulted in a sizable amount of resentment and hostility toward her boss. Now the plot becomes even more convoluted: As a way to demonstrate disapproval of her boss, the executive assistant would translate directives to subordinates in a manner which would give them the impression that they were being demeaned and "talked down to."

For example, if a housekeeper had a problem or was in conflict with one of her peers, she would naturally gravitate toward her Spanish speaking supervisor. This rendered the Executive Housekeeper's "open door" policy useless. This became very clear to everyone but

Men's natures are alike;

It is their habits that separate them.

~ Confucius

the General Manager and the Executive Housekeeper, who was really running the show in this department.

Any organization can fall victim to these kinds of dis-ease elements. However, all of this confusion, back-biting and substandard service could have been avoided. All that was needed was for people to communicate directly with one another, in a professional manner. If the Executive housekeeper had taken the time and made the effort to learn basic "Hotel Spanish" her staff would have gained respect for her efforts to bridge the language gap, and would have had no reason to go to anyone else in the Department if they had a major concern or complaint.

Also, had the general manager been doing his work correctly, he would have been aware of the fragmentation between these two department heads long before operations became disjointed. He could have then sat with both of them and "laid down the law" about the need for direct, open and professional communication. Yet nothing of the kind ever materialized. What started out as a minor issue involving a "failure to communicate" ballooned into a major dysfunction involving two large hotel departments.

Ethnic & Racial Divisions in the Workplace

This situation had its root causes in a failure to properly and professionally value ethnic & racial diversity. There are many instances where a failure to engage in a well thought out approach to working with diverse racial and ethnic groups can spell disaster for an organization.

The most heinous example I've ever seen of a complete devaluation of a racial group occurred in yet another hotel setting. This time, the setting was in a suburb of Detroit. Because the auto industry was booming at the time, most anyone who wanted to work could find a

Resolve to be thyself, and know that he who finds himself, loses his misery.

~ Coventry Patmore

job in one of the many car plants in the region. This was not a good thing for the area hotels, who relied on "cheap labor" to staff their lowest paid positions, like housekeepers and line cooks.

The solution they came up with was to use an outside firm to contract immigrant labor, in this case African males, to work mostly in the janitorial and housekeeping areas. As it turned out, these fellows were excellent workers who carried with them wonderful dispositions. But the level of racial bigotry demonstrated by the majority of the "official staff" toward these immigrant laborers was, to say the least, abominable.

My services were contracted not to address these issues. In fact, I had no knowledge that this situation even existed. Rather, my assignment was to "improve the effectiveness of front desk and administrative operations." It didn't take long to find out how truly dis-eased this place really was. My initial interviews with staff were marked by an unusually high level of suspicion and mistrust. In the minds of staff, I was just an antagonistic "outsider" who came to "change things." No one, it appeared, wanted things to change. Everything "was just fine, thank you!" By day three, I wasn't sure if I was in a hotel or apartheid South Africa. I had never seen an operation that harbored so many hidden agendas or so much racial bigotry.

Every individual I encountered, save for the Africans, who were considered "contract labor," were negative to the point of being obnoxious. In order to gain a clearer perspective of what was going on, I decided to spend a morning with these outside laborers helping them clean rooms. They were extremely hard working. But more than that, they were happy people. Happy to be alive, happy to be earning money to feed their families and happy not to be starving. Although I spoke limited French, which was the language they all understood, I discovered many of them spoke several languages which were indigenous to their respective countries. They smiled, big toothy smiles, as

The tragedy of a man's life is what dies

inside of him while he lives.

~ Henry David Thoreau

they recited poetry, sung songs ... and cleaned toilets. What a great bunch of human beings! Yet, within the confines of this hotel, they were nothing more than "low level laborers," not worthy of even a passing hello.

When I brought up the subject of refusal to integrate any of the contract labor into hotel activities, such as recognition of birthdays, or small cash rewards for great service, I was told by the General Manager that, "these people aren't 'real' employees. And what's more," he intoned, "none of them speak English." By the end of the week, I had had quite enough of this "Heartbreak Hotel." Racial bigotry, favoritism, authoritarian control, lack of sound business ethics, absence of team work, devaluation of employees, lack of confidentiality—in short, a litany of dis-eases—permeated every part of this operation. It came as no shock to learn that this was the poorest performing hotel in the company's region. Everybody was devalued. The Africans, however, were the worst of the lot.

I submitted my assessment report, with full knowledge that I had no intention of doing any "piecemeal" damage control. It was either complete, top to bottom overhaul or nothing. No band-aid cures for this place! My report was accepted, and the fee paid. Nothing more was said. A month later, both the General Manager and Assistant General Manager had resigned. Several months later, a company insider mentioned that the hotel was up for sale.

The intriguing thing about this case study is that while the dis-ease conditions were extreme, the reason for the hotel's demise had more to do with financial loss than with dysfunction. I've seen first hand examples of dis-eased companies that continued to make a profit, and, as a result, the troubles contained in their operations would be completely dismissed or, at worst, given the old band-aid cure. In the example just cited, caveats were made about how certain condi-

When your thinking rises above concern

for your own welfare, wisdom,

which is independent

of thought, appears.

~ H.A. Gakure

tions might fester, resulting in disastrous consequences. However, the policy was to ignore all warnings and continue "skipping through the tulips" until the ink on the company's ledger turned bright red. By then, it was time for major surgery.

Informal Leadership

As we look at various case studies of dis-ease, the notion of poor leadership has emerged as the primary cause of performance nose dives. Yet there are subtle aspects of organization life that often act to help or hinder leadership efforts. In any business there are people who have natural abilities to influence others. Not all of them are managers or executives. Oftimes significant degrees of power and influence reside within the non-supervisory ranks. Through a combination of personal charisma and an ability to capture an understanding of the fundamental needs of their associates, informal leaders contribute enormously in shaping the attitudes and behaviors within an organization.

People who become informal leaders can sometimes wield more power and influence than their bosses. Within Fleet Management operations, it was the informal leaders who determined both the pace and quality of work performed. Likewise, in our pathetic Detroit hotel, it was informal leaders that stoked the fires of fragmentation and racial prejudice. Even in companies with unions, informal leaders often tip the scales of decision making, over and above the presence of any existing union structure. In troubled businesses, where strong leadership is lacking, informal leaders are capable of exercising more influence than most managers or executives.

Informal leaders operate in "parallel formation" to official managers. Within Fleet's management, the informal leaders would take directives from official supervisors and decide how, or if, these directives

*When people are serving, life is
no longer meaningless.*

~ John Gardner

would be carried out. The importance of informal leaders cannot and should not be underestimated. These leaders can be both help or hindrance to the growth and stability of the business. The strategic question is, how do you deal with them? The simple answer is to involve them directly in projects or decision making. For example, if there is a change initiative underway, informal leaders can assist in making these efforts successful.

There are also times when informal leaders can be given formal leadership responsibilities. This has the effect formalizing their accountability and shaping the scope of assignments, as well as coaching them about expected desired outcomes. In addition, it's also a lot easier to track their activities to evaluate performance levels. I don't at all mean to imply that informal leadership is intrinsically bad. It's just helpful to know what this leadership is thinking and how in tune they are to what the goals and aims are of the management team.

In the presence of bad management, informal leaders assume the role of a "Greek chorus," letting you know that your bad management is not going unnoticed. However, there are times when informal leaders use their status to pollute well-intended management initiatives. Once again, it's management's responsibility to constantly take the pulse of their line staff to determine how they're shaping up in the minds of the rank-and-file.

If informal leaders are undermining operations, as we saw earlier in our computer sabotage example, then it is up to management to remove these destructive elements as quickly as possible. A distinction must be drawn about what "undermining" really means. When good leadership is absent and no real direction exists, informal leaders become critics that are well worth listening to. In these instances, informal leaders are merely echoing back the sentiments of their peers. Dis-eased businesses are notorious for not listening

Everything I did

in my life that was worthwhile

I caught hell for.

~ Earl Warren

to what's "blow'in in the wind," to paraphrase Bob Dylan. And more often than not, the wind is blowing from the mouths of the informal leadership.

Informal leaders are not always aggressive "nay sayers." In a dispirited casino I once consulted for, it was characteristic of the rank-and-file employees to feel that no one was paying attention to them. There was, however, one crusty, hard working black jack dealer who doubled as a kind of priest/counselor to all of those troubled souls in table games. I made a point to get to know him because he seemed open and forthcoming in talking about what was not working on the casino floor. He, himself, was content to do his job and go home. In both manner and style, he was passive. Yet, he had extensive knowledge and keen insight into what wasn't working in his service area. His role as an informal leader grew in stature because he was genuinely empathetic to his co-workers, who by themselves, had difficulty coping with the poor management they were subjected to.

People naturally gravitated to this fellow, openly sharing their discontent. He was both an attentive listener and a seasoned counselor. Very few casino managers were aware this dealer had such a strong influence with his peers, and even fewer recognized how his good advice and easy manner averted potentially hostile confrontations between managers and subordinates.

As is typical with most people of his character, he had no interest in entering the managerial ranks. Because of his innate understanding of the personnel dynamics of the casino, he had a strong distaste for what he saw as a corrupt system. In his eyes, too many people rose to management positions because of "brown-nosing" with higher ups. He felt that managers were always caught up in "company politics," which he had no time for.

Love your enemies just in case your friends

turn out to be a bunch of bastards.

~ R.A. Dickson

Eventually, after leading a major change initiative toward more effective management, I persuaded our reluctant informal leader to chair an employee task force. This quiet "nay sayer" was now in the position to become directly involved in helping this severely dis-eased table games operation. He rose to the occasion with flying colors!

The important lesson to grasp in this story is this: within every business there exists certain informal leaders who, if identified and empowered properly, can provide immeasurable assistance in helping to re-shape dis-eased operations. To allow these individuals to go unidentified is to lose a potentially invaluable resource for positive change. Too many people, who under certain circumstances would make outstanding managers, go unnoticed by "ignor-ant" bosses. It's a tragic waste of human resources, and a gross strategic error.

When a manager or supervisor labels someone a "nay sayer" or "troublemaker," it's vital to investigate the circumstances which resulted in the labeling. There are, indeed, real troublemakers out there. They come to work everyday with one intention: to destroy anyone or anything they don't like, by whatever means. However, you must make certain that their intentions are malevolent before action is taken. Identifying informal leaders, gaining an insight into how they think and assessing the validity of their views is a tried and true method for gaining a clearer insight about potential sources of dis-ease within a company. At times, the "virus" dwells within management, and other times, the sickness is one of a failure to attend to proper communication with staff. Whatever the reason, understanding the attitudes of informal leaders is a way of learning about the inner workings of a company. This information, which is both overlooked and undervalued, is critical in helping to shape a strategy which involves rather than alienates personnel.

When informal leaders function in similar operational surroundings an "informal hierarchy" is formed. In one of my career "incarna-

Do not fear death so much

as the inadequate life.

~ Bertolt Brecht

tions," I served as assistant to the Secretary of a southwestern state's Department of Health. This civil service organization was bloated by hoards of "less than on purpose" employees. They all understood the intricacies of exploiting the system. For example, they knew that it was almost impossible to be fired after moving successfully through a probationary period.

This knowledge, together with lots of idle time, turned some of these state employees into first class troublemakers. (With all due respect, most Health Department staff were quite well intentioned—even if they didn't have a particularly good work ethic. Generally, their days were spent reading the newspapers, taking extended lunches and standing in hallways talking about how many years they had left before they could retire. Sometimes they reminded me of prisoners chatting about how much time they had left to serve out their sentence!)

There were a few individuals who noticeably stood out from the rest. Their level of vicious intent was palpable. These individuals were particularly hostile toward anyone who tried to plow through the bureaucracy to get things accomplished. Managers who were appointed, and did not go through the standard civil service hiring procedures, became particularly juicy targets for these "state employee assassins."

I once suggested to my boss, the Secretary, that we should change the job titles of these bona fide terrorists to represent what they actually did to earn their paycheck. Some of the suggestions included: "Senior Back Biter," "Apprentice Shit Disturber," "Saboteur Analyst" and "Character Assassination Specialist 1 & 2." The presence of just one of these individuals made daily work life a real challenge. One well placed saboteur could eat up hours of one's work day. Under such circumstances, managers tried to do the best they could, in the hope that one of these conspirators might step in front of a speeding Mack truck or merely retire gracefully, never to return again.

Please give me some good advice in your next letter. I promise not to follow it.

~ Edna St. Vincent Millay

This is an example of an informal hierarchy at its worst. The system literally stymied any attempt to manage and direct people effectively. In retrospect, the only effective way to deal with these serpentine creatures, given the limitations of the state government system, was to be a "super leader" and rally the troops around a common cause, motivating people at every step.

This I attempted to do with a modicum of success. The downside of these efforts was complete physical and mental exhaustion, which was a direct result of the excessive amount of time that was required to prod various operational components to set goals and enforce accountability. Taking careful baby steps, in the hope of moving incrementally forward, can be a very frustrating activity. In my short tenure with state government, I saw dozens of extremely bright, capable people leave government service—the direct result of the system's inability to adequately correct poor performance and enforce high levels of accountability. Workers were only held accountable for being a warm body, in a fixed place, for a fixed time. High standards and top notch performances did exist, but these were only aberrations floating on the surface of a sea of ineptitude and lethargy.

Even though government operations can be mired in red tape and saddled with a less than enthusiastic work force, they can be made more responsive through relationship building. In the absence of an ability to effectively discipline or terminate poor performers or disruptive individuals, these systems can still be positively impacted through the sheer strength of winning people over—with fairness, challenging assignments, effective team building efforts, group decision making, fun activities outside the workplace and a number of other tactics that can be introduced independent of the stagnant system that the operation is contained in.

Use your weaknesses;

Aspire to the strength.

~ Lawrence Olivier

Information Gaps

In such difficult settings, managers must make a concerted effort to develop a "shoulder-to-shoulder" rapport with their subordinates. One of the ways to accomplish this is to carefully evaluate how communication flows within the operational environment. In this regard, the Japanese have already broken solid ground. They've created a place in their well ordered pattern of social harmonization for both criticism and debate. When someone in a Japanese business introduces a proposal (called a *ringi*) it is passed up and down the corporate ladder. At each level it must receive a stamp of approval, or a *han*. A proposal may have dozens of *hans* before the plan is activated.

Western businessmen perceive Japanese businesses as slow moving. But in reality, a lot is going on behind the scenes. And much of it is intangible. The process they employ allows people to spend time developing strong relationships. For executive managers, this means giving themselves free reign to filter through all levels within the operation to get an accurate sense of the strength of support that exists for company-based initiatives. This constant nurturing of positive human relationships means that once the business, as a whole, makes a final decision, the plan has everyone's sincere support.

The process does have a slow moving beginning. However, before long, action becomes swift and precise—making continuous questioning unnecessary. With information moving freely, it's no wonder that many of the best action items and proposals emerge from middle and lower company echelons. The very nature of management is changed by such a process. Rather than hide proposals and plans from workers, they are laid bare for debate and criticism. Because this "style" of information sharing is so transparent, the role of managers is transformed from one of control to one of striving to achieve consensus. In this model, it's the senior

When the eagles are silent,

the parrots begin to jabber.

~ Winston Churchill

managers who have the responsibility for both assimilating information and setting goals.

It's the manager's job to prove the nay-sayers wrong or accept the validity of their criticisms and make the necessary changes. The idea is to create a more open place for dialogue, one where ideas and criticisms can be discussed in a professional manner, without any attending back-biting or lowering of individual self esteem. Good ideas and positive input can't be generated in environments that are authoritarian or overly bureaucratic. These examples of Japanese business styles are far from perfect. Yet Japan, despite its recent years of economic downturn, does have models that are worthy of consideration.

Japanese as well as Europeans seem to be much more conforming in their allegiance to hierarchies than in North America. Here, we must act more conscientiously to win "the hearts and minds" of employees. Both the proof and the pudding must be one and the same. Sadly, this is the exception rather than the rule in American business. What you see and hear from management is not always what you get. The net result of this "honesty gap" is the growth of dispirited workers, whose loyalty declines steadily as the information gap widens. The other negative aspect about a less-than-open pattern of information flow is that it breeds attitudes and behaviors that can easily degenerate into behavioral dysfunction.

Much like our democratic system of government, which fosters the illusion of universal equality, American enterprises operate with an illusion that the "whole" is coherent and solid, with the standard motto being "we're all one team here." The recent scandalous debacles at ENRON, WORLD COM and numerous other corporate giants, which arose from excessive greed and hubris in high places, and which is linked with the 500 to 1 ratio of corporate CEO and worker earnings, suggest that inequity is a commonplace feature of

One day, who knows? Even these hardships

will be grand things to look back on.

~ Virgil

business in America. Responsible managers need to begin to correct these inequities or face a back lash that will result in disastrous consequences for our economy. It's highly improbable that a work force will demonstrate much allegiance toward a corrupt hierarchy.

This "imbalance," once again, is a direct result of withholding information from people. To achieve real success, companies need to thoroughly evaluate how information is transmitted up and down their organizational ladder. This is no easy task. In large operations, middle managers and supervisors are often the communication messengers for the company. They are given responsibilities for carrying information both upward from line staff and downward from the top execs. In many instances the messages are highly distorted, for any number of reasons. In the hands of mediocre or inferior middle managers, even well intended messages can become mangled and subject to misinterpretation.

I was once asked to assist a business in dealing with its acquisition of a rival firm. Ironically, both businesses were physically located next to one other. After several months, a number of thorny issues involving tenure, salaries, benefits, etc. were resolved, apparently to everyone's satisfaction. Each staff largely remained untouched after the acquisition, save for a substantial overhaul of upper level managers. Operationally, things stayed much the same. Yet, after a short while, the "newly acquired" employees started to noticeably lag behind their counterparts in performance and accountability. The "parent" company thought this was strange, because they felt the acquisition provided the old company's employees with better wages and benefits. What could the problem be?

At first, little information was shared. Employees felt the acquisition would be better for them in the long run. "After all, it was a bigger company with better benefits." Then, in small trickles, the cause of

We take our shape,

it is true, within and against that cage of

reality bequeathed to us at birth;

and yet it is precisely through our

dependence on this reality that we

are most endlessly betrayed.

~ James Baldwin

the malaise was revealed: The employees were suffering from information deprivation. They had a number of questions on their minds that they felt needed answering: Because their equipment was old and outdated, would it be replaced? Would they get to work in the other, more modern building? Would it be possible to sit on certain employee committees? Also, they wanted to share information about several procedures they used before the acquisition, which they thought would work better than the ones the new company had imposed. Could they discuss these procedures with management? As one might guess, these people were hungry for dialogue.

Despite their sincere appeals, no answers were forthcoming. Why, I wondered? Further inquiry finally put some "meat on the bones." I discovered that the parent company's supervisors were not given any information related to the questions raised by the employees. Equally important was the fact that the line supervisors didn't bother to tell their bosses about the questions these "new" employees had raised. No information was flowing up the pipeline, and none was flowing down.

As the information gap widened, uncertainty in the ranks grew, and with it, a flourishing rumor mill. A sharp decline in productivity and morale quickly followed suit. Here's the essential point: People find it hard to work in an information vacuum. If they don't get information, they'll invent it. That's when the infamous "Rumor Mill" takes over. Show me a company with a strong rumor mill, and I'll show you a company that has a debilitating dis-ease. And if that dis-ease is left untreated, it could prove to be life threatening.

This situation demonstrates the danger inherent in major communication gaps. One gap arose as a result of the failure of the new management to engage in shoulder-to-shoulder dialogue with the newly acquired employees. (What a great opportunity for internal PR!) Yet,

Many of life's failures

are people who did not realize

how close they were to success

before they gave up.

~ Thomas Edison

months after this acquisition was formalized, the silence coming from management was deafening.

True, certain issues and procedures were ironed out. But, what then? It was clear that the parent organization had failed to bring these new employees into the fold. However, as I soon discovered, the enterprise wasn't doing such a good job involving their long term employees in meaningful information exchange, which is most likely the reason why the supervisors did not take their subordinates' messages back to senior management. They knew that little information would be forthcoming, and anyway, as one supervisor commented, "why stir the pot?"

The Perils of Navigating Change

The damage that resulted from this lack of shared information most probably had no "evil origin." It was rather the result of a bad case of chronic mediocrity. The company did not see the importance of getting their managers' fingernails dirty by infiltrating the ranks with their knowledge, openness and goodwill—unfortunately, they felt there were better things to do. *The dynamics of change is such that fear about one's future is uppermost in the hearts and minds of those most impacted by the change.* Businesses often don't take into account the fear factor that change places on individuals. The changes can be minor, yet they still produce anxiety and apprehension.

During my tenure with state government, I had the opportunity to witness, first hand, an extreme example of how minor changes can generate tremendous anxiety. Following some minor restructuring, it was decided that desks should be rearranged to accommodate the influx of new staff. As it turned out, the desks of several employees were moved away from the large window where they had been positioned. This was immediately interpreted as a sign that these employ-

The only way to avoid being miserable

is not to have enough leisure to wonder

whether you are happy or not.

~ George Bernard Shaw

ees were being "targeted" by upper management—that an attempt was being made to "squeeze them out of their jobs." Nothing of the sort was happening. However, this extreme example of employee paranoia does emphasize the degree to which people will infer the worst when change is in the air.

Similarly, downsizing often produces much residual anxiety for those remaining on the job. The loss of friends and co-workers, in and of itself, is equivalent to witnessing the death of one's colleagues. Also, the concern arises: "Oh, God, Am I next?" Usually, while this undercurrent of fear is playing itself out, the company is giving "pep talks" about how work must continue in an uninterrupted fashion. At a time of extreme loss, it's business as usual. This type of managerial approach is shortsighted and ultimately damaging.

An incident once took place involving a local bank in my home town, which was being taken over by a larger bank. Because of the takeover, many of the bank's activities were now carried out by corporate headquarters, which was located far away in another state. Nearly half of the banks' employees were declared "redundant" and were subsequently asked to leave. How did the new parent company handle this loss of local talent? They threw a big party!!

I walked into the new/old bank celebration, only to be greeted by grim-faced employees handing out balloons and grape juice. I asked one teary eyed teller what was going on. She said, "We're having a party because we've just become the Bank of such-and-such." "You don't look too happy," I replied. "Oh, I know.... I guess I need to smile," was her answer.

Some questions come to mind. What kind of assistance did the employees who were laid off receive? Was any counseling offered either to those staying or those leaving? What kind of "transition pro-

It's alright to have butterflies in your stomach.

Just get them to fly in formation.

~ Dr. Rob Gilbert

gram" was put into place following the new bank's takeover? How did new management mediate the morale issue, in light of the loss of so many staff members? What was the level of trust, loyalty and commitment engendered from employees as a result of the takeover?

I did a little homework, and discovered that the takeover was abrupt. No real transition program was put into place. All information was disseminated in a series of impersonal "memos." There appeared to be little or no opportunity for questions by any staff member. Only one formal meeting was held, and this was a rather "cut and dried" affair. Employees who were let go received letters detailing their date of departure and final salary arrangements. Period. End of paragraph.

What can be said of these actions? Yes, they were cold, harsh and emotionally painful. But for whom? Certainly, for the people who were let go. But what about the individuals who were "lucky" enough to survive the purge? How were they affected? What kind of loyalty or devotion to duty do they now feel for this new corporate boss? What is their trust level? Was anyone from the new Bank asking these questions? Apparently not.

Chances are, the remaining employees are performing their jobs more out of fear and concern for their own self interests than for any feeling of positive identification with their new corporate employer. Yes, one could argue that downsizing and acquisitions are part of life in today's business world, and that letting people go is a "business decision," pure and simple. However, if a company really wants to create a work force that's committed and energized, it must take into account the psychological impact that change and loss have on employees. Granted, it's no fun to lose your job under any circumstances, nor is it a great experience to see close colleagues dismissed.

But the way in which a company engineers such changes determines the messages that employees internalize. These messages are then

I don't want any "yes men" around me.

I want everybody to tell me the truth

even if it costs them their jobs.

~ Samuel Goldwyn

projected outward to families, friends and the greater community at large. When this takes place, will the messages be ones of support or ones of dis-ease?

Once in a while, a business will really work hard to plan smooth transitions for employees hit with takeover or downsizing. But these instances are exceptions. Given the rapidity of some acquisitions and downsizing activities, there's often little quality time to prepare employees for sudden changes in their status. However, to do nothing is to plant germs for long term dis-ease within the company's human resource infrastructure. In the long run, this lack of "response-ability" from executive management produces destructive outcomes.

When I first began consulting work, I could sense the pride that employees had for the their companies. Now-a-days that same pride and sense of loyalty is significantly harder to find. The reason is apparent: Employees no longer believe their company is working with their best interests in mind. In today's business world everything is subject to change. Even amidst this constantly shifting landscape, developing mechanisms for open communication and information exchange can position an organization to both withstand the rigors of internal and external change and to strengthen its ability to become a high performance enterprise. Like everything about change management, it's all in the identification and implementation of details. These details emerge from working closely with employees at all levels to find out how they feel and what they need.

Turfs in the Workplace

In discussing the issue of communication and causes of organizational dis-ease it would be a great omission not to talk about "turfs" in the workplace. Turfs exist when parts of the organiza-

There is only one way

to achieve happiness on this terrestrial ball.

And that is either to have a clear conscience

or none at all.

~ Ogden Nash

tion declare themselves, in subtle or overt ways, to be "off limits" to other parts. Attempts to find out what's going on or what isn't working in another turf are typically met with hostility, threats, rebuke or plain silence.

When thinking about turfs, the musical "West Side Story" comes to mind. Over on this block live the Jets, on the next, the Sharks. The two exist side by side as contentious foes, each protecting their physical boundaries, each defending them from potentially hostile intruders. To enter into a rival's turf is to openly court trouble. When individuals from rival turfs try to bridge ideological gaps and negative perceptions that one turf has for the other, they themselves run the risk of being harmed.

Spend time in any dis-eased business and you'll shortly meet members of the Sharks and Jets. However, they might not call themselves by these names. Rather, they refer to themselves as Accounting, Marketing, Sales, Administration, Legal, Merchandising, and the like. They may resemble one another in appearance, but that's where the similarity ends. They carry with them different sets of priorities, agendas, goals and objectives. When threatened, they excel at naming, blaming and shaming—tools designed to deflect a turf member's need to be accountable. People who reside in turfs are usually well aware that probing too deeply to expose the "dirty linen" of another turf might backfire, requiring them to expose their turf to similar scrutiny. Consequently, hiding dirty linen is one of the primary strategies of any loyal turf member.

Turfism embraces an attitude which says "don't cross this line." It perpetuates a "them" versus "us" mentality and fosters an allegiance to certain parts of of the organization over other parts. It funnels communication down blind allies and through complex mazes, causing confusion and disarray.

The superior man understands what is right;

the inferior what will sell.

~ Confucius

Turfs generate misinformation and harbor feelings of separateness. They produce feelings of contempt and bitterness from "outsiders." Also, turfs force other parts of the business to navigate around issues rather than dealing with them directly. If turfism does all these nasty things, why do companies tolerate them?

A good part of the reason is power. Turfs are formed and maintained by people who either have power or are perceived by others to have it. Remove the power source, and the turf will disintegrate. That's not always easy to do, however—especially if the "leaders" who broker power are in a position to expose weaknesses of colleagues in other parts of the company. In such instances, a pervasive attitude on the part of non-turf members which says, "it's best to mind our own business," prevails. Turfism, like other dis-eases which plague the workplace, attacks healthy, open communication, which directly influences the capacity to think and act strategically.

Real leadership emerges when there is a recognition that allowing turfs to exist is unacceptable. That action takes courage and involves risks. One false step, and you might fall victim to "turf power." It's important to understand that turfs function to protect collective self interests. Businesses cannot hope to be nearly as successful as they might be when various components within the enterprise function as fragments rather than seamless entities in relation to one another. Nevertheless, the presence of turfs in businesses is often ignored or downplayed by management, much to the detriment of the company and everyone in it.

Sometimes rival or competing turfs go to war—just like street gangs. When they do, more time is spent warring than working. Everyone in a turf war becomes a potential victim—even innocent bystanders get caught in the crossfire. In some companies turf wars become a way of life. The Chamber of Commerce case I referenced earlier is an

The hardest thing to learn in life is

which bridge to cross and which to burn.

~ David Russell

outstanding example of an on-going turf war that hindered operations for years. As new employees came on board, part of their "informal" orientation was to become familiar with who belonged to what turf, and how one should maneuver through it so as to insure survival. To the unknowing observer, everything seemed to be functioning well in this organization. However, this was all just smoke and mirrors. In reality, very few inter-departmental contacts went smoothly. In the world of turfs, illusion becomes reality.

The Problem of Power Cliques

Turfs should not be confused with another fragmented dis-ease entity, the so-called "power clique." A "clique" is defined as "a small, exclusive group of friends or associates." The key word here is "exclusive," because by definition, cliques exclude people who might otherwise make positive contributions to the business. Power cliques tend to control information and decision making. However, only information and decisions that are important to the power clique will get attention. Matters which don't effect their spheres of authority or interest are usually ignored.

Power cliques are inherently political. They're more about maintaining control than shaping policy or building sound business philosophies. Like turfs, power cliques are generally self serving. They are elitist because they fail to involve people outside the clique, who might make valuable contributions toward the decision-making process.

Power cliques can exist at any level within the business—from line staff to upper management. They usually exert influence when an issue of personal concern or a matter involving control is at stake. To quote a phrase from an old college professor, their involvement depends upon "whose ox is being gored." Like turfs, members of power cliques exist

It's motive alone that gives character

to the actions of men.

~ Jean de la Bruyere

to support each other in retaining positions of influence or control. Attempting to enter a power clique is highly political. Competing elites can waste valuable time, money and energy as they compete for power.

I experienced the workings of a highly effective power clique during an assignment with a business school. The school was being criticized by the national association responsible for accrediting schools of business. The accreditation agency expressed concern that the graduate curriculum did not conform to the associations guidelines, as it pertained to course offerings and curriculum structure.

As a result, they were in danger of being placed on probation. The Dean contacted me to try and establish a working consensus to support certain changes which would satisfy the association's guidelines. At this juncture, the reader needs to consider the uniqueness of academic structures: Their system of granting professors "tenure for life" is both archaic and stultifying. Tenured professors typically teach only one or two classes a semester and spend the rest of their time (supposedly) doing research and writing. If it weren't for the intense back-biting and petty politics, academic institutions would be ideal places to work. Instead—more often than not—they are loosely knit structures containing a potpourri of malcontents, egoists, eccentrics and an occasional honest scholar or two.

In many graduate schools of business, the environment lends itself to doing a fair bit of outside consulting. This is not necessarily a bad thing, provided that the primary attention is focused on assisting students to grow into knowledgeable, ethical business professionals. Unfortunately, I have not seen many examples of this. Systems of accountability in academia are somewhat amorphous, to say the least.

Given this crazy quilt structure, I was not surprised to find an absence of tenured professors on my various fact finding excursions within

Think nothing profitable to you

which compels you to break a promise,

to lose your self respect, to hate any person,

to suspect, to curse, to act the hypocrite,

to desire anything that needs walls

or curtains about it.

~ Marcus Aurelius

this institution of higher learning. Granted, faculty did post office hours, but for the most part, the hallways were like an old west ghost town, with a scattering of administrative support staff, so as to provide some semblance of life.

I began a process of interviews to find out how the school operated. The Dean painted a picture of all kinds of behind-the-scenes power plays by people wanting to dethrone him. He gave some particularly grisly examples of self-serving attempts to undermine his plans for a more responsible curriculum. Basically, the interview provided me with the Dean's "bird's eye" perspective of all the bad guys that were causing him grief and disrupting the growth of the school itself.

I decided to talk to some of the players the Dean had criticized. All of them, without exception, were tenured colleagues. From them emerged a different picture. The Dean, they claimed, wanted to monopolize power. He didn't want to listen to the judgments of the various committees of the business school faculty. They claimed he was a master of withholding information and a self-serving opportunist.

In an effort to create some degree of consensus and move toward the goal for much needed reform, I decided to create a task force, whose job would be to evaluate how the school's curriculum could be broadened and made more appealing to a wider range of students. These actions were consistent with the recommendations of the accrediting association. Try as I might, I could only enlist a fragment of tenured faculty to be regular members of this task force. Some of the bolder junior faculty, whom I found to be intelligent, motivated and supportive of the task force's aims, formed the majority of members.

As the meetings progressed, I found myself doing quite a bit of back stage politicking. I discovered that the real concerns of the tenured professors had very little to do with building a solid curriculum.

Life's most urgent question is

what are you doing for others ?

~ Martin Luther King, Jr.

In a nutshell, they were preoccupied with having their ego-based needs met. Because none of their jobs were threatened, they could have easily used their combined intellects to work synergistically to develop a stimulating, innovative program.

Instead, their interests, for the most part, were petty and mundane. One fellow was concerned about losing a faculty slot in his particular area to another "rival" area. This was disturbing to him because the professor who headed that area had criticized one of this fellow's publications, calling it "second rate." Another tenured observer, who was not a task force member, would periodically step in to meetings and create confusion and upheaval. I soon discovered that he was on the tenure committee which would decide the fate of many of the task force's junior members.

After months of hard work, the task force finally drafted a well crafted proposal that did represent a more balanced curriculum. I was proud of the work they had done. It was a real accomplishment, under less than ideal conditions. I was informed that this proposal would be brought to the general faculty for a vote at its next meeting.

Traveling off to another assignment, I returned a week later to discover that the proposal had been voted down. Once the real showdown took place, various tenured faculty, all of whom had an ox or two that would have been somewhat gored, should the proposal have passed, spoke out against it. In order not to jeopardize their chances for tenure, most of the junior faculty either abstained from voting or voted "nay." This diverse assortment of power brokers had stepped in to thwart positive change, so as not to in any way force them out of their comfort zones. The real victims were the business students themselves, who, once more, had to plow through a curriculum that had the potential of being much more stimulating and diverse. They deserved better.

Success on any major scale

requires you to accept responsibility ...

In the final analysis, the one quality that all

successful people have is the ability

to take on responsibility.

~ Michael Korda

The Confines of Culture

The patterns of dis-ease outlined in this book all possess a common characteristic: self interest. Individuals that pursue self interests, to the exclusion of what is best for the organization, are planting seeds of divisiveness and inefficiency into the soil of the enterprise.

Realistically speaking, organizations are far from perfect. At times, indeed, things do go wrong. This is quite natural. However, the important question that must be asked is, "How committed is the enterprise to solving its problems?" Experience has led me to believe that the answer is "not terribly." More often than not, companies seek solutions that are not really designed for the long term. We saw this when we looked at the "band-aiding" efforts in the hotel examples.

Perhaps this has something to do with not wanting the shareholders to get wind of the fact that "something might be rotten in the state of Denmark," to quote Hamlet. The ability of management to recognize the presence of dis-ease and join together with a minimum of ego investment, determines how forward moving, flexible, open and innovative a company is in its desire to be healthy and profitable.

The true variable that determines a business' "response-ability" to internal dis-ease lies within its "culture." Culture is an interesting concept. The dictionary defines it as the "totality of socially transmitted behavior." Let's try and decode that concept through a simple illustration: I've noticed that when I go into my neighborhood bank, at least one or two tellers are always chewing wads of gum. Curious guy that I am, I asked a teller one day what the policy was concerning gum chewing.

She looked at me strangely. "What d'ya want to know?" she replied. "Well," I continued, "Are you allowed to chew gum at work?" "Oh,

A person's errors

are the portals of discovery.

~ James Joyce

yeah," she responded, "nobody ever says anything about it, so I guess it's OK." It would then seem that because "nobody said anything about it," it means that anybody working in the bank, at any time, can chew gum. On another trip to the same bank, I noticed that one of the personal bankers was working at her computer and—that's right—was chewing gum! On subsequent visits, I noted that many people were gum chewing. Therefore, I concluded that gum chewing is a socially acceptable part of behavior for employees at this bank. In other words, gum chewing is an acceptable part of this organization's culture. I later discovered that there was a policy that did not permit gum chewing. However, it was never enforced. So, apart from what the "formal rules" were, gum chewing was an accepted part of this bank's culture. The point is, culture determines behavior. As such, it has a greater impact on attitudes and values than any formal set of rules or regulations.

Let's look at another example: One day my fax machine died. I went to a local business equipment "Superstore." The fax machine I wanted was not in stock. It had to be ordered. I was told that it would take about five days to arrive. I asked the store clerk if they could telephone me when it came in. He said he could. Seven days passed and I had heard nothing. I decided to give the store a call. "Hold on," the voice said curtly. Several minutes later, after enduring some less than appealing techno music, the voice at the other end said, "Yes, we have the machine. It's been in for a few days." "Really," I said, "OK, I'll pick it up later this afternoon." I hurried over to the store, which was only several blocks from my office.

"Hi, I'm Barry Cooney. I'm here to pick up my fax machine." The clerk asked me my name again. "Barry Cooney," I said, spelling out the last name. He went to the computer. "Yes, we have it, but it's over at our warehouse, you'll have to go pick it up there." "What!"

Nothing splendid has ever been achieved

except by those who dared believe

that something inside them was

superior to circumstance.

~ John Barton

I shouted. "The warehouse is on the other side of town. I only live two blocks away from this store!" "Sorry, you'll have to pick it up at the warehouse." Needless to say, I was not too pleased. Canceling my order, I resolved never again to do business with this place. Weeks later, I learned from friends and acquaintances that customer service at this store was hit-miss at best. Additional horror stories confirmed that at this business superstore, the customer was always wrong. I later learned that every employee at this store was required to go through a formalized customer service training. Yet, this store had a terrible reputation for service delivery. Their training program said one thing, but their culture reinforced another.

Had they been willing to go the extra mile and deliver the fax to the store where it was ordered, I would have overlooked the incident. However, dis-ease was so much a part of this business' culture that customers left in droves.

When business cultures go bad, tinkering with parts of the operation will do little good. There are scores of well-intended managers who spend ninety percent of their time putting out fires as a result of flawed internal cultures. They continue doing this day in and day out with no likelihood of appreciable positive change. Excessive fire fighting is a sign that the organization's culture has a severe, contagious dis-ease. In instances like this, major surgery is required to restore health to the operation. Asking each employee to take two aspirin and retire for a good night's sleep won't make things better when the sun comes up the next day.

What makes a culture dis-eased? There's no single answer to that question, save to say that *when maladaptive behaviors continue to go uncorrected, they eventually become embedded in the fabric of the organization and, in time, are viewed as normal.* As the clerk at the business equipment superstore said, in response to my continued

It's not the size of a dog in a fight,

it's the size of the fight in the dog.

~ Kit Raymond

protests, "that's how things work around here." It would have been more accurate for him to say, "that's how things *don't* work around here." I never cease to be amazed at how dis-eased business cultures can become before anyone gives a thought about taking some action. Imagine a company that has authoritarian managers operating in an environment of fear and mistrust. Imagine further that decisions within this operation are made by various groups of power cliques in the presence of other groups of people who are members of various turfs within the company. Add to this toxic stew the presence of low paid, disempowered line staff, whose loyalty to the enterprise is questionable, at best. And what do you have? If your answer is, "a portrait of my company," you are not alone. This pattern is ubiquitous in business settings.

Bringing about positive cultural change within a business environment is a multi-faceted process. Policies and procedures must be closely aligned with behaviors and attitudes. There need to be opportunities for people at all levels of the business, to contribute ideas and share input about what a dynamic work culture looks like. Attempts must be made to demonstrate that management is deeply concerned about creating a healthy internal culture. Managers must make sincere efforts to become active role models in this process, and make it known that people who have no intention of supporting the new culture must find other employment—no if's, and's or but's!

Internal PR, in support of the new culture must be put into place, so that everyone knows that building a new culture is top priority. Lastly, there must be a reasonable time frame to test the strength of the new culture and evaluate how things are going. For larger organizations, one to two years is not an unreasonable period for a cultural shift. The important thing is doing it right and making it last.

This then is the human problem;

there is a price to be paid for

every increase in human consciousness.

We cannot be more sensitive to pleasure

without being more sensitive to pain.

~ Alan Watts

Organizational Wounding and Its Symptoms

An important factor that the organization must also consider when attempting to re-make the culture is the degree to which the work force has been stigmatized by the old culture's dis-eased elements. I call this stigmatization "organizational wounding." Employees, at all levels, have the potential to become "wounded." The wounding is primarily a psychological phenomenon. It occurs over time and is caused by constant exposure to poor leadership practices which are embedded within the dis-eased framework of the business culture.

For instance, the wounding might start to attach itself to the individual's psyche when he witnesses colleagues being unjustly fired, when policies and procedures make life on the job difficult or when he feels excluded in decision-making processes. The reasons for becoming wounded are almost limitless. Organizational wounding affects both individuals and groups. Here are some symptoms to look for:

A. *Marked Cynicism Toward Change*

In this case, the employee has witnessed a number of failed attempts to bring positive change to the organization. As a result, both the employee's receptivity and capacity for buy-in become limited. This means that the focus and intention necessary to make the change initiative happen never took place, despite the "hype" surrounding the initiative. When past initiatives have not worked, the cynicism surrounding productive change can be quite intense. The probability that this cynicism will spread to more passive or mildly receptive workers is high. Much direct, no-nonsense discussion needs to occur in order to carefully articulate what kind of change is being attempted and what is expected from all concerned.

Hold yourself responsible for a higher standard

than anyone else expects of you.

Never excuse yourself.

~ Henry Ward Beecher

B. *Inherent Mistrust Of Management*

An organizationally wounded individual lacks confidence in his bosses. He has lived through too many instances where the "upper rungs" of management grossly failed to "walk their talk." Nothing uttered by management is taken at face value. Every memo or pronouncement is subject to scrutiny, and carefully analyzed for hidden meanings or covert implications which may be interpreted as being threatening to certain individuals or groups. Eliminating or substantially reducing feelings of mistrust is time consuming. Many small victories need to be won for the momentum of mistrust to reverse its course. Honesty and direct, clear communication are the basic tonics that are required.

C. *Difficulty Working as a Team Player*

To be organizationally wounded is to be in constant survival mode. Defensive posturing becomes the primary form of response to any directive or mandate. In this state, the employee is innately suspicious of colleagues and finds it difficult to share information or lend full cooperation to any group activity. Rather than assist in developing consensus, the organizationally wounded employee tends to carry with him his own agenda, which he overtly or covertly seeks to impose on others. Once again, constructing a clear vision for change and utilizing tools to bring people together is the way to proceed.

D. *Loss of Creative Energy and/or Ability to Think "Outside the Box"*

Somewhere along the line, the employee has made attempts to be creative or think "outside the box." These attempts have been muzzled or thwarted by the company's culture, supported by myopic, plodding management practices. Disappointment, anger and

Make your work

to be in keeping with your purpose.

~ Leonardo Da Vinci

discouragement have gradually given way to acceptance of the status quo. Numbness and indifference have replaced any desire to try new things or critically assess existing practices. Simply stated, there is not much "juice" available for problem solving or creative thinking. This form of wounding is particularly destructive to the enterprise—the reason being that, on the surface, everything appears to be moving along, the usual moans and groans of dissatisfied workers are seemingly absent. Lurking beneath the surface, however, is a collective sense of despair, a kind of "organizational ennui" that bears a lot of resemblance to an individual who is chronically depressed, but still manages to somehow get through the day. The solution here involves nothing short of a cultural re-make within the operation.

E. Lack of a Sense of Ownership and Responsibility

The organizationally wounded person perceives herself as vulnerable. She seeks to diminish her sense of responsibility and ownership for any task or assignment. She attempts to divert attention to herself by continually "finger pointing" and blaming others for mistakes, inconsistencies, or short-comings. She is quick to criticize others and equally quick to construct endless excuses for why things aren't going well. Responding to this form of wounding entails creating new ways which individuals can become aligned with one another—sharing purposeful activities in an atmosphere of mutual support. More about this will be said in Part II.

F. Negative Attitude Toward the Workplace

A wounded employee carries with him a negative attitude toward his workplace. Because of pent up frustrations, this type of response reflects a narrow and somewhat intractable view of the operation in general. In this context, trivial matters become disproportionally disturbing. Complaining becomes an obsessive preoccupation, and pes-

The love of truth lies at the root

of much humor.

~ Robertson Davies

simism becomes lodged in almost every thought and activity related to the business. There are times when this feeling is so intensely felt, that no amount of change will "cure" the dis-ease save for a complete job change. The organization that seeks renewal must be patient with people like this—but only to a point. When others start the shift toward positive attitudes and behaviors, retaining "die-hard" pessimists is not the most desirable strategy. However, every wounded employee deserves to be given the opportunity to become part of a forward moving initiative. Keen judgment is required as to when the business needs to "cut bait" and send these wounded (and angry) employees packing.

G. A High Probability for "Burn-Out"

Psychologically wounded people can develop lots of health problems. Headaches, backaches, muscle pain, sleep disturbances and depression are not uncommon symptoms for those working in dis-eased settings. Burn-out is often the result. This form of burn out is different from the kind of burn out that besets some "Type A workaholics," who place enormous stress on themselves to perform better and achieve more than their peers. Burn-out through organizational wounding is a slow, insidious process, a process which doesn't always reveal itself until there is an emotional or physical collapse. When good people burn-out they need a bit of quality time to recover. So much of burn-out manifests as a result of feelings of over-load, lack of support and underappreciation. The company can take steps to correct all of these conditions if it is sincerely interested in retaining good people.

If we were to view these characteristics as describing a single employee, we'd probably agree that this person is not contributing a great deal to the success of the company. However, dis-eased organizations, by definition, create wounded employees, many of whom possess one

Our sincerest laughter with some

pain is fraught.

~ Percy Shelley

or more of the characteristics just described. The result of this barrage of negative stimuli is a hoard of wounded souls, who wittingly or unwittingly spread the ailment to their peers. As such, organizational wounding is a highly infectious disease. As the Arab saying goes, "He who walks with the lame, will become lame." No wonder that any business which has a sizable number of wounded personnel is one that moves with a very bad limp. Businesses must be prepared to seriously look at the "wounding factor" as they attempt to bring life back to an ailing operation.

And Now a Pause for a Lighter Side of Business Dysfunction

A colleague was kind enough to forward me, via email, some examples of internal company communications containing glaring warning signs that dis-ease is lurking just beneath the surface. I doubt that these items are contrived; they certainly do appear to resemble similar situations that we've all observed. Some of these communications are humorous, others are not. No matter. As you read them, think about what kind of woundings or dis-eases might exist in these work sites..... or in your own. Here they are:

Company Wide Memo

"As of tomorrow, employees will be able to access the building using individual security cards. Pictures will be taken next Wednesday and employees will receive their cards in two weeks."

A man isn't poor if he can

still laugh.

~ Raymond Hitchcock

From an Accounting Manager

"Email is not to be used to pass on information or data.
It should be used only for company business."

From an R & D Supervisor

"No one will believe you solved this problem
in one day. We've been working on it for months.
Now, go act busy for a few weeks and I'll let you know
when it's time to tell them."

From a CIO of a Major Computer Company

"My boss spent the entire weekend retyping a 25-page
proposal that only needed corrections. She claimed the
disk I gave her was damaged and she couldn't edit it.
The disk I gave her was write-protected."

From a Shipping Executive

"My sister passed away and her funeral was scheduled
for Monday. When I told my boss, he said she died on purpose
so I would have to miss work on the busiest day of the year.
He then asked if we could change her burial to Friday.
He said, 'That would be better for me.'"

A story should have

a beginning, a middle, and an end ...

but not necessarily in that order.

~ Jean Luc Goddard

<u>*From a Supervisor from a Division of a FORTUNE 500 Company*</u>

"We know that communication is a big problem,
but the Company is not going to discuss it with employees."

<u>*From a Communications Director at a Major Fast Food Corporation*</u>

"As Director of Communications, I was asked to prepare
a memo reviewing our company's training programs and
materials. In the body of the memo, in one of the
sentences, I mentioned the 'pedagogical approach' used
by one of the training manuals. The day after. I routed
the memo to the Executive Committee, I was called into
the office of the Director of Human Resources, and told that
the Executive Vice President wanted me out of the building
by lunch. When I asked why, I was told that she wouldn't
stand for perverts (pediphiles?) working in her company.
Finally, he showed me her copy of the memo with her demand
that I be fired—and the word 'pedagogical' was circled
in red. The HR Manager was fairly reasonable, and once he
looked up the word in the dictionary and made a copy of the
definition to send back to her, he told me not to worry. He
would take care of it. Two days later, a memo to the entire
staff came out directing us that no words which could not be
found in the local Sunday newspaper could be used in
company memos. A month later, I resigned. In accordance
with company policy, I created my resignation memo by
pasting words together from the Sunday paper."

New organs of perception

come into being as a result of necessity.

Therefore, O Man, increase your necessity

so that you may increase your perception.

~ Jallaludin Rumi

Part Two

Strategy Number One:
Ending Workplace Dysfunction Through
Dynamic Leadership

"Leadership is the daring to step into the unknown."

~ Stephen Hawking

This investigation of dis-ease within organizations is essentially an exploration of the "human side" of business. It concerns the nature of valuing people in the workplace and the effect that increasing de-valuation has in destabilizing the work force. It is an exposé of human-based factors which can cause a business to under-perform, to the point of dis-integration.

Examples of business dis-eases are endless. I'm sure that, in addition to the ailments I've been discussing, it would be possible to compile a list of dysfunctions which are peculiar to certain industries or fields

Rest not! Life is sweeping by;

Go and dare before you die.

~ Johann Wolfgang Von Goethe

of study. Yet, dis-ease elements such as authoritarian management, dishonesty, lack of empowerment, turfism, power cliques, avoidance of responsibility, character assassination, etc., transcend specific job categories. Because of their universal nature, we can easily recognize these destructive characteristics. Trying to call them something other than a dis-ease or a dysfunction is equivalent to putting lipstick on a bulldog—it doesn't make him any prettier.

However, knowing that these corrupting elements exist in our working environments is not good enough. They're simply too destabilizing to be ignored. In a recent survey conducted by a research firm in Indianapolis, only 24% of the respondents said they were committed to the company they work for; only half said they would recommend their employer to others seeking employment. Given the dis-ease factors we've been investigating, is there any doubt why these percentages are so lopsided?

The question now before us is: "What can we do to eliminate these dysfunctional dis-eases?" Let's first look at the type of leadership that needs to be in place to properly address the dis-eases that have been outlined thus far.

It's possible to spend your entire life reading about leadership and remain unable to lead effectively. If we look at figures like Napoleon, General Patton, Abraham Lincoln, Gandhi, Winston Churchill, Henry Ford or scores of other dynamic leaders, we quickly become overwhelmed by their "bigger-than-life" personalities. Understanding the lives and historical contexts of these and other great leaders doesn't necessarily help us discern the subtleties of dealing with situations that involve unmotivated employees, self-centered supervisors or managers defending their turfs.

Leadership in business can be quite confusing. And it can become even more puzzling when you factor in all of the peculiarities of the

Neutral men are the devil's allies.

~ Edwin Chapin

company's culture. One thing is certain: troubled businesses have an over-abundance of dis-eased managers who are only going through the motions of leading. After wading through all sorts of definitions of leadership, I've arrived at a simple one:

Leadership is the ability to influence people
to achieve certain desired outcomes.

That being said, the question becomes "How DO you influence people?"

In the 1940's there was a bank robber, Willie Sutton, who received much notoriety. The police would capture him, and then he'd escape—again and again. Willie had quite a colorful personality and liked talking to the press. One of Willie's famous responses to the question, "Why do you rob banks?" was "Because that's where the money is." In addition to this oft quoted pronouncement, Mr. Sutton is known for a less famous quote, "You can get more with a smile ...... and a gun, than just a smile." When I think about Willie's statement, the word "gun" stands out in my mind.

It's apparent that the gun represents brute force: For example, if I ask you for money, you may or may not give it to me. However, if I point a gun to your head, you're much more likely to comply—quickly, without argument. Sadly, the business world is populated by multitudes of managers who try to get things done by holding a gun to people's heads. This is nothing more than management by fear, intimidation and threat. The tactic is not only ineffective, it's counterproductive.

Today's modern work force needs to be able to "run with the ball" without having someone looking over their shoulders, prodding them with loaded pistols in hand. Employees need to feel a level of commitment which allows them to willingly identify and solve problems before they spin out of control. They need to feel an inherent trust

It is not only what we do, but also what we do not do, for which we are accountable.

~ Moliere

in both the company and its management to provide clear direction. They need to believe that fair treatment is an overriding concern of the business. They need to directly experience being part of the action—that their views and ideas really do matter, that they legitimately feel valued in their work. These feelings can never develop in places which use threat and intimidation to get things done.

Even the presence of a few management "intimidators" can poison the well. Allowing "bullies" to run your operation is like putting anthrax spores in the ventilation system—everyone quickly succumbs to the disease. As a graduate student, I remember being surprised at the notion put forth by one of John F. Kennedy's political advisors, Richard Neustadt. He claimed that presidential authority was based more on persuasion than power. He went on to say that when dealing with powerful figures like the head of the Joint Chiefs of Staff, the FBI Director or the director of a large labor union, it was more the art of persuasion than adherence to presidential authority that produced desired outcomes.

Using persuasion as a leadership tool doesn't imply that the leader is "soft." Persuasion functions as a more effective tool than crude "strong arm" tactics when linked to a set of ethical "guiding" principles. When strong guiding principles become the back bone of leadership, the leadership initiative itself is buttressed by a sense of integrity. The act of leading with integrity is more of a unifying force than leading with force or duplicity. Integrity has staying power.

Leadership shouldn't be confined to the upper tiers of management alone. On the contrary, it needs to be be cultivated throughout the enterprise. The difference between designated leaders and people given leadership roles lies in the concept of "span of control." Consider these examples: a mail room clerk leads an initiative to make improvements in the way mail is handled, a dishwasher speaks up in

What you say

tells other people what you are.

~ Anonymous

a task force meeting to talk about how people in the kitchen can demonstrate more teamwork, a mid-level supervisor takes on a key role in spear-heading a company-wide initiative. All these activities demonstrate leadership, yet their span of control is circumscribed by specific objectives that may be of limited duration or significance.

Every one of these examples required leadership. For the average employee, the opportunity for developing a real sense of loyalty and buy-in is intimately connected to the value given him by assuming leadership roles such as the ones described above, even though they are limited in design and scope. Creating committed employees becomes crucial when businesses must respond rapidly to internal or external change. In these uncertain times, the need to deal with change has become commonplace. A disempowered work force that is given little "response-ability" will respond in kind when asked to alter established way of doing things.

Over the years, I've heard many CEO's and other executive manager types complain about employees who don't pay enough attention to details. The standard line is, "If it was their business, they wouldn't allow such and such to happen." By denying line staff an opportunity to perform in certain leadership capacities, it's unrealistic to expect any sense of ownership to occur. In the absence of a sense of ownership, numerous things that need attending to will be neglected. And when front line employees start to neglect things, the company becomes susceptible to all kinds of "dis-eases."

Characteristics of Leadership

The inherent challenge in talking about leadership is that the capacity to lead is filled with intangibles. There is no one personality type that can be cited as the paragon example of what a leader should look like.

Stay present.

You'll always have time to worry

later on if you want to.

~ Dan Millman

However, there are a number of descriptive behaviors and attitudes that can help shape a leadership profile. In a way, each characteristic blends with the other, making elements of one inextricably connected to the other.

For the purpose of clarity, let's look at these characteristics as separate entities, knowing full well that they are all part of the same unfolding fabric. In order to get the most out of these descriptive characteristics, take some quality time with each of them. While doing so, try to reflect upon the following questions:

How naturally do these characteristics fit my personality?

What kind of effort must I make to bring out these behavioral and attitudinal elements?

How do I begin to express them?

Leadership, especially in dis-eased enterprises, requires a special kind of energy and focus. Take a careful look at yourself and observe how these characteristics "resonate" with who you really are. Then, ask yourself if you're prepared to take on the responsibility of a leader in a dysfunctional setting.

1. Leaders need to have a strong determination to lead.

"Our doubts are traitors, and make us lose the good we oft win by fearing to attempt."

~ William Shakespeare

Perseverance is a great element of success.

If you only knock long enough

and loud enough at the gate,

you are sure to wake up somebody.

~ Henry Wadsworth Longfellow

Determination means "firmness of purpose." You can't be effective by leading people halfheartedly. If you truly want to lead, you have to mean it. This requires developing a commitment to put into play behaviors and attitudes that enable you to influence others. Players in dis-eased organizations tend to not be followers. This is because of the pessimism that has accrued over time—much of it directed toward their designated leaders. This is why any would-be leader in a troubled organizational setting must be an individual who has the focus, energy and intention to lead. Without this intention, potential followers will quickly try to carve out their own behavioral and attitudinal path.

There's a story about Albert Einstein told by one of his assistants at Princeton. After having finished a research paper, Einstein was looking for a paper clip. All he could find was one that was too badly bent for use. He searched for an implement to straighten it. After opening up drawer after drawer he came across an unopened box of clips. Seeing it, he removed one clip and shaped it into a tool to straighten the bent one.

His assistant was puzzled, and asked him why he was doing this when he now had a whole box of unused clips. Einstein replied, "Once I become set on a goal, it becomes difficult to deflect me." It's that very kind of determination and purpose that is required to fuel the leadership drive.

Leaders must be open to learn from both mistakes and failures. It's the determination to move through failure that enhances a person's leadership status. Oswald Avery, the Canadian bacteriologist who discovered DNA as the basic genetic material of the cell, conducted hundreds of failed experiments, yet his determination to find solutions to complex genetic questions was monumental.

It is more important to find out what you are giving to society than to ask what is the right means of livelihood.

~ J. Krishnamurti

Commenting once on a string of failed experiments, he said, "Whenever you fall, pick up something." True leaders, pick up all kinds of information from their mistakes—and remain resolute in their determination to succeed.

It's imperative for leaders to convey a sense of determination in all that they do and say. Followers will be less willing to support a leader if there's not a high level of concordance between words and deeds. Walking the talk and talking the walk creates a strong foundation for leadership. What the walk and talk consists of determines the scope of the leader's vision. Every spoken word and every action should ideally become a model for others to follow. It's not an easy thing to do. That's why our companies are filled with so many managers and so few leaders.

In troubled companies followers are always placing managers under a microscope. This is because one of the primary dis-eases in businesses that aren't functioning well is mistrust and lack of credibility. If a manager can hurdle these obstacles they have a chance of assuming a leadership role. Such a role carries with it a strong mandate to change things for the better. Managers can't hope to do it. Only leaders can.

The kind of leader I am describing seldom wavers. Although at times it may become necessary to stop and consider the success of one's strategies and be prepared to chart a new course if results are not solid. Nonetheless, the determination to succeed remains constant. Any person who wants to lead needs to ask themselves a few honest questions:

How determined am I to be an effective leader?

What are the underlying reasons why I want to lead?

What personal characteristics or habits do I need to let go of to lead people effectively?

Moral courage and character go hand in hand. A person of real character is consistently courageous, being imbued with a basic integrity and a firm sense of principle.

~ Martha Boaz

In my youth, I spent a great deal of time immersed in classical music. I had the good fortune to be exposed to many brilliant musicians, most of whom played with the Philadelphia Orchestra. I looked with wonder and admiration at their musical mastery.

Observing them as teachers, I came to realize that the driving force behind their musicianship was a deep and profound love of music. Their determination to develop their artistry originated from this deep seated attachment to their instrument, the sound it produced and the thrill of combining that sound with other sounds produced by an array of different instruments.

Leaders who merely want to exercise power and control aren't operating with these kinds of higher purposes. Metaphorically speaking, they are not looking for a blending of "instruments and sounds." Dominance is their main objective, at whatever cost. This kind of "power monger" no matter how effective he seemingly is, has the capacity to do great harm, simply because his ultimate goal is to remain firmly in control.

Lord Acton's famous principle, "Power corrupts, and absolute power corrupts absolutely," fits this argument well. If your determination to lead is based on a sincere desire to improve not just your company's P&L statements, but the quality of life of those who use your products and services, then you're on the right track. Otherwise, your leadership objectives are essentially corrupt and disharmonious.

A determination to lead should be linked with a concurrent wish to deal with any personal habits or behaviors that blunt leadership effectiveness. For example, people who don't listen well or who are quick to anger have some serious personal work to do. In dis-eased companies, big egos and personal self interests abound, making effective leadership initiatives more "dis-ease prone." Navigating through the

By your thoughts you are daily,

even hourly, building your life;

you are carving your destiny.

~ Ruth Barrick Golden

toxic waters of dysfunction requires an ability to listen to all points of view and make decisions that are fair and just, without causing extensive fragmentation or discord.

When one is convinced that assuming leadership feels comfortable, and once a serious appraisal of the reasons behind one's decision has been made, an important first step has been taken. Now the Game begins.

2. Leaders must uplift people with positive attitudes.

"Your living is determined not so much by what life brings you as by the attitude you bring to life; not so much by what happens to you as by the way your mind looks at what happens."

~ Lewis L. Dunnington

The ability to think positively and transmit that positive energy to others is an enormously powerful leadership tool. Used in the right way, reflecting positive attitudes can move mountains. Mark Twain once said, "Life does not consist mainly or even largely of facts or happenings. It consists mainly of the storm of thoughts that are forever blowing through one's mind." You're in a much more commanding position to lead if the thoughts you invoke are ones that inspire, motivate and energize. The implications of this should be apparent—positive thinking results in positive behavior.

The philosopher William James hit the nail on the head when he said, "The greatest discovery of my generation is that a human being can alter his life by altering his attitude of mind." Reading this quote, I am reminded of Shakespeare's play, *Henry V.* King Henry is about

Nurture your minds with great thoughts.

To believe in the heroic makes heroes.

~ Benjamin Disraeli

to go to battle with the French. His army is outnumbered five to one—not the best of odds. But Henry rallies the troops with an amazing speech, in which he says, in part:

> *"For he today who sheds his blood with me,*
> *shall be my brother; be he ne'er so vile*
> *This day shall gentle his condition: And*
> *gentlemen in England, now abed Shall think*
> *themselves accurs'd they were not here,*
> *And hold their manhoods cheap, whiles any*
> *speaks That fought with us upon St.Crispin's Day."*

Strong words. Strong enough, in fact, to inspire Henry's outnumbered army to defeat the French. I'm not implying that to be an effective leader you have to be a great orator. Not by a long shot. Positive attitudes can change behavior in simple, yet significant ways.

For example, I used to go to a neighborhood deli every morning following my exercise work out. Each day I'd encounter a gruff, mean spirited, unsmiling woman behind the counter. After a while, her routine was predictable: she would slide my buttered onion bagel across the counter, and turn her head immediately to the next customer with no comment and no eye contact.

The bagels at this deli happened to be the best in town, but the service was just awful. After a while, this lady's grim presentation made the bagel I was eating seem far less appetizing, so one day I decided to try an experiment. I was going to attempt to change this woman's behavior by being sincere, polite, upbeat and engaging. Every morning I made a point to call this counter person by name, look directly in her eyes, smile, say good morning, ask her how she was doing and

A man is about as happy

as he makes up his mind to be.

~ Abraham Lincoln

wish her a great day. Every morning I'd go through the same routine, and every morning I'd get a few inaudible "grunts" in reply.

At some point in this process, I noticed she was engaging in some eye contact. One day she even muttered what sounded like "you're welcome," in response to my "thank you." Then, quite unexpectedly, a dramatic shift took place. After missing almost a week of exercise because of a bad cold, I went back to my old routine and returned to the deli for my usual onion bagel and coffee. As soon as I entered, the counter woman blurted out, "Where have you been? I've been missing your big smile!" Then we began to talk. I discovered that she had a son who had died just two years before in an auto accident.

Steadily, she began to open up, and after a while, became almost cheerful. I began to notice that I started receiving more than the average amount of cream cheese on my daily bagel. Eventually, I started joking with her about the bagels being so good I dreamt about them. She replied, "that's because they're love bagels—they're made with love." From that point on, I would always put an order in for a "love bagel." Entering the store one afternoon, I was greeted by the counter woman with what had now become her usual smile, "I know," she said, "one love bagel coming up."

A dour-faced man standing next to me suddenly looked up. Sensing the good vibes, he intoned, "Yeah, gimme one of those love bagels, too; I could use it." I can't be certain whether it was my actions alone that altered this lady's demeanor. However, my gut tells me that my efforts had a significant influence in changing her "attitude paradigm."

It's a fact: Positive attitudes create positive energy. When both are sincerely expressed, old unproductive responses give way to more open expressions and feelings. I have no doubt that positive attitudes have the potential for generating enthusiasm. Charles Schwab once noted,

Life is either a daring adventure -

or it is nothing.

~ Helen Keller

"A man can succeed at almost anything for which he has unlimited enthusiasm." The responsibility of a leader is to help produce that enthusiasm. Without it, energy dissipates and pessimism grows.

In dis-eased businesses, positive attitudes have the potential for reducing anxiety and allowing people to begin to more objectively comprehend the nature of the difficulties which plague them. Positive thinking, then, is another important tool in the leader's toolbox. In combination with other tools, a uniquely powerful opportunity for overcoming obstacles is realized.

One of my very special mentors was a gentleman named Albert Carlo. His friends called him "Count Carlo." The Count had many talents. He was an accomplished painter, an interior designer, a writer, a "Scrabble Player Extrordinaire" and an amazing entrepreneur who could bring groups of talented people together by virtue of the sheer power of his personality. Carlo lived through the Great Depression of the 1930's. He frequently found himself almost penniless, yet he always managed to live and eat reasonably well. He told me once about an event that took place during this time.

Late one afternoon he ran into a friend on the street whom he had not seen in several months. Knowing that the friend was in a much better financial condition than himself, he asked for a small loan. Owing to the gravity of the times, his friend reached into his pocket and handed Carlo a five dollar bill, which, at that time, was worth quite a lot. Whereupon Carlo immediately went to a top men's clothing shop and bought a bright red silk handkerchief which he promptly displayed in the front pocket of his suit jacket.

"Why," I asked, "would you ever spend that kind of money on a silk handkerchief?" "For several reasons," he replied. "First and fore-most, it made me feel good. Secondly, it highlighted my appearance

Go out on the limb -

that's where the fruit is.

~ Will Rogers

because people were drawn to the bright red silk fabric. In a way," he continued, "the silk handkerchief represented success, and people are much more willing to support successful people than to give hand-outs to losers."

Count Carlo understood the value of both positive thinking AND positive symbols. He felt, looked and acted successful; as a result, people treated him that way. Through positive thinking, Carlo fulfilled his own prophesy of abundance. As the book of *Proverbs* states, "As a man thinketh in his heart, so is he." Positive thinking is a highly potent health tonic. People in sick companies yearn to drink it—and, they seek out others who dispense it. In their heart of hearts, they really want to be a healthy person in a healthy work environment.

The Count was a wise and knowledgeable mentor. He understood that people are drawn to positive energy, particularly people who are worth knowing. Because of this understanding he had scores of close friends and associates who assisted him in his entrepreneurial endeavors throughout his long career. Reflecting on this phenomenon, Carlo would smile, take a puff of his cigar, gaze upward and exclaim, "Life provides."

Albert Carlo knew from deep within that in order to uplift people, he first had to uplift himself. Carlo did this on a daily basis, and the positive returns were inexhaustible. Pause for just a second. Think about those people in your life who've inspired you. What did they do to make this happen? What was it about their characters that generated this positive effect? How has their influence effected you—up until this very moment? What kinds of energies or feelings must you recapture to renew this energy? Asking yourself these kinds of questions will assist you in your efforts to uplift yourself and others.

Bear in mind that leadership is an unfolding process. Grasping this process by looking deeply into these and other leadership characteris-

Nothing is terrible except fear itself.

~ Francis Bacon

tics will move you farther along as a decisive leader. Curing dis-eased organizations requires an exact form of personal inquiry. You must know yourself and your intentions to lead people, particularly those who are caught up in dysfunction and uncertainty. There are no short cuts in becoming an authentic leader.

3. Leaders must learn how to deal with fear.

"Fear is the main source of superstition, and one of the main sources of cruelty. To conquer fear is the beginning of wisdom."

~ Bertrand Russell

Fear is defined as "a feeling of agitation and anxiety caused by the presence or the imminence of danger." My experience as both a therapist and business consultant has confirmed over and over again, that fear is the most debilitating form of dis-ease. For leaders, the inability to mediate their fear and the fears of others is a sure-fire formula for failure. Fear gives rise to a host of counterproductive feelings and emotions: doubt, uncertainty, hesitation, depression, lack of clarity, impulsiveness, anxiety, inconsistency, duplicity, disloyalty, discomfort, inaction. All are rooted in fear.

The curious thing about fear is that most of the time, it is groundless. Psychologists know that if people think they are in danger they will experience fear, regardless of whether a real and present danger actually exists. If, for example, I think that a hungry pack of wolves are on the other side of my flimsy cabin door trying to break in, I'll respond fearfully, triggering a number of probable responses: sweating, rapid breathing, accelerated pulse rate, dilated pupils, dry mouth, rapid heart rate and body tremors. I might also begin to think illogically and

The only thing I am afraid of is fear.

~ The Duke of Wellington
(The "Iron Duke")

start to panic. All of this is part of the "fight or flight" response that will kick in when danger is thought to be present.

In work situations, it's not easy to run away or fight when fear arises. Instead, flight might take the form of trying to blend into the woodwork, not speaking out when unfair actions take place or deflecting responsibility onto others. Expressions of the fight component might entail explosive anger, inappropriate remarks, self-protective behaviors or taking revenge.

Tragically, some people's entire lives are ruled by fear—a fear that is the product of thought alone. Most try to cover it up, but beneath the surface, fearful thoughts erode the ability to perform with clarity and purpose. Once this inaction sets in, the ability to face challenges and work well under pressure is sharply reduced. Fear of "not being good enough" or of "making a mistake" are two of the most common business fears. Leaders can help allay these kinds of feelings by providing solid training and personalized coaching, as well as by fostering an attitude that allows for mistakes without the anticipation of fearful consequences.

At this writing, I'm practicing the Japanese form of drumming known as *Taiko*. *Taiko* drumming involves precise ensemble playing. Playing drums in the *Taiko* style entails movements that resemble those in the martial arts. Although I've become a fairly decent amateur hand drummer, exposure to the disciplined techniques of *Taiko* initially created within me an avalanche of fear. Knowing this, my initial thought was to abandon *Taiko* and return to the more relaxed style of Latin percussion, where mistakes are easier to hide.

However, our instructor has a way of washing people's fear away. His approach is, "Don't worry about the choreography, don't worry about missing beats or making mistakes—just move, play, have fun." In between the playing and having fun, he good naturedly shows us

To him that is in fear

everything rustles.

~ Sophocles

the complex techniques that are employed. In a short while, I found myself playing with an accuracy and quality that I'd never thought possible. Why? Because the fear component was removed. In the absence of fear, I could do things that my fearful mind said were much too challenging. Removing fear from the workplace would, in one fell swoop, boost productivity and lower costs to the tune of millions of dollars, and, in the process, infuse businesses with a vital new work ethic. Overnight, we would make all the struggles to "re-engineer" and "reorganize" far less relevant.

To mediate fear, a leader must also be a teacher. As a teacher the leader helps to create positive attitudes about how the experience of work needs to be perceived. Such efforts help to remove the fear that most people have about performance. This concept relies heavily on building a supportive environment where employees no longer feel that their work life is about merely "covering your butt." At its highest level, leadership transforms individual fear into a willingness to work closely with others in the pursuit of collective goals and objectives. The act of joining with others in cooperative efforts is an effective mechanism for dissipating fear of failure.

When people are encouraged to share experiences, what were previously called "mistakes" now become opportunities for collective learning. You know that a company has reached such a plateau when the content of meetings shifts from "how somebody screwed up," to a discussion about a valuable group learning experience. How often have you attended meetings with that kind of format? Sadly, most regularly scheduled meetings are merely "white-wash" sessions in which everyone tries to diplomatically avoid talking about "dirty linen." As the saying goes, "meetings are events in which minutes are taken and hours are wasted."

To get to a place where people are honest and open in handling mistakes and failures requires changing the fabric of the business

Everyone and everything around you

is your teacher.

~ Ken Keyes, Jr.

culture. This means addressing the issue of accountability in much broader terms. In other words, how does the business evaluate collective performance? What responsibility does the "collective" have in determining the success of the individual? What beliefs does the company support relative to rewards and recognition of groups as well as individuals? All of these questions have a bearing in determining how an employee looks at herself and what she does. When it comes to questions of responsibility, is the employee nothing more than an island unto himself? What kinds of built-in support systems exist to link individual self-worth with a larger collective identity, where victory for one implies a victory for all?

The way in which a business answers these questions determines the type of work paradigm it embraces. Usually, organizationally wounded employees operate in a framework wherein support systems are quite fragile—if they even exist at all. In most companies you can't necessarily count on your co-workers to stand behind you when things go wrong. The more performance is linked to individual activities, the greater the probability that "wounding" will occur. And as we've seen, there is a direct relationship between being fearful and feeling wounded.

Effective leaders seek to expose underlying causes for employee fear and apprehension and, in so doing, develop systems that allow for more shared responsibility in the way work activities are configured. This is one way a leader mediates fear in relation to subordinates.

Facing the Hungry Bears

Thus far, I've been attempting to outline work-related fears that are the products of fearful thoughts alone, without any legitimate basis other than past experiences and conditioning. However, there are times when internal or external conditions produce legitimate

Courage is grace under pressure.

~ Ernest Hemingway

concerns about the business' ability to grow and prosper. In these instances, fear is more than just the mind imagining dire consequences—real challenges must be faced. How do we, as individuals, deal with fear?

On a trip to Istanbul, I found myself walking down a narrow, poorly lit, cobblestone street. The street was in the "Old Quarter" of the city. It was riddled with deep pot holes making walking somewhat challenging. You never knew if you would fall into some muddy rut or trip on a jagged piece of stone. After a few minutes, I sensed the presence of someone walking behind me. I didn't hear the actual sound of footsteps, yet the impression that someone was behind me was intense.

Turning around abruptly, I saw something that, at first, I couldn't believe: a natty-haired bear wearing a muzzle with a blue ribbon around its neck. Although it was clear that the bear wasn't fully grown, its huge claws convinced me that I could quickly become his evening snack, if he had the urge. I quickened my pace, not wanting to break into a full stride, fearing that it might signify panic and prompt an attack. My heart started pounding. At the same time, I was beset with thoughts about how absurd it would be to be killed by a bear on a back street in Istanbul—what was even worse was the fact that I had left my passport back at the hotel. If I were killed, no one would know who I was. I decided that panicking wouldn't do any good, but I had to think fast. Then something unique took place. Even though I was afraid, I determined that I was not going to meet my end by being a helpless victim.

Interestingly, as soon as I made this resolution, I began to think more clearly. I became aware of the fact that just ahead of me was another narrow street running perpendicular to the one I was now on. This street looked like it had a bit more lighting, and, given where I was in the Quarter, the street might even open up to a major thoroughfare. I

Life shrinks or expands in proportion

to one's courage.

~ Anais Nin

began to construct a plan: I would continue to walk at a brisk pace; and when I reached the other street, I would cut a sharp ninety-degree turn and run like the blazes. It was a move I had perfected with much success in back alley touch football games while growing up in Philadelphia. After devising this strategy, I felt more confident. I was still scared, but now there was hope.

Once again I glanced over my shoulder to see what the bear was up to. He had responded to my quickening pace by moving more rapidly. Nose in the air, he appeared to be closing the gap as each second passed. I readied myself for my ninety-degree pivot. Just as I was about to bolt down the side street, I heard a human voice shouting in a language that I did not recognize.

Turning around, I saw a man—who appeared to be a gypsy of some sort—making sweeping gestures with his arms. I then caught a glimpse of a bigger bear that was standing next to him. This, no doubt, was Mama, and the smaller one trailing after me, her offspring.

Hearing the shouting, the smaller bear who was on my heels, turned in the opposite direction and broke into a full stride toward Mama, who was waiting patiently at the other end of the street. As quickly as the drama had begun, it ended. The terrifying fear of being killed by a bear and my resolve to not give up without some kind of resistance was now history. This incident has remained with me for many years—not just because I was grateful to have survived, but as a testimony to my resolve in the face of my impending demise.

Now, in times when I feel afraid, I see in my mind's eye the image of that natty-haired bear with the blue bow around his neck; and along with that image, I experience a visceral feeling of resolve, a resolve which says, "Yes, I WILL survive." None of us have to let fear cripple us. Leaders need to carry with them this sense of resolve—a resolve

A man of courage is also

full of faith.

~ Cicero

which says, "We will do whatever is required to conquer external threats to our survival and continued growth." When a leader is able to effectively communicate this conviction, a positive group synergy ensues. As we all know, there are many "hungry bears" lurking in the dark alleys of the business world. The leader's job is to teach followers not to become attached to the fear of being eaten, but to the exhilaration of becoming smarter and more strategic than one's adversaries. Strangely, many fears that have work-place origins are extensions of people's fear about death.

Once during a workshop with sales people, I spent an entire afternoon discussing fear. I pointed out that from a psychological perspective, the fear of not making one's "quota" is linked to a fear of job loss, which, in turn, is related to a fear of not being able to support oneself. And when there is no money to support oneself, there is no money for food. Without food you will starve. And, of course, starvation eventually leads to... death. So, hidden in the dark recesses of the mind, the fear of not making a sale is equated to that ultimate fear—the fear of death.

Crazy as it sounds, this is the sequence that often lies behind the fear of not being able to meet sales quotas. Michael Pritchard summed up the nature of fear nicely when he said, "Fear is that little dark room where negatives are developed." And the kind of negative thinking that surrounds fear in the workplace is always sequential: first this will happen, followed by this, then this, etc., etc.

Rather than physical death, prolonged fear in one's work environment can lead to a far more damaging experience—the death of the soul. Clinging on to life in a dis-eased company is much like losing one's soul. Individuals who take on leadership roles must be prepared to assist employees to move beyond the limitations caused by their fear of not succeeding.

No amount of skillful invention can replace the essential element of imagination.

~ Edward Hopper

Dealing with fear in an organization is subtle at times. It involves building up the confidence of both individuals and groups. It also entails creating a "Vision of Success," one that encourages people to move beyond their individually-based doubts and apprehensions. It means allowing the collective to become part of something that transcends their own feelings of limitation.

Job-related fear is as common as the the common cold. People who have developed these fears are often individuals who have experienced the loss of their jobs. Transcending this fear involves a sense of resolve—that through shear force of will, coupled with a vision of success, obstacles can be hurdled.

Walt Disney once said, "If you can dream it, you can do it." As such, leaders must also be dream makers, in the sense that they are able to harness the power of imagination into actions which produce visible accomplishments. Those in leadership positions must be able to convince followers that through collective effort any and every challenge can be overcome. But in order to do this, the power of fear that cripples one's efforts and motivation must be conquered.

That's not an easy assignment, especially when it concerns the fear that workers have in relation to change. As was mentioned earlier, just moving desks around in a state government health office was enough to spread fear throughout the building. Because dis-eased companies have such high levels of fear, effective managing of change can be difficult.

Effective leaders must first manage the fear that people have about change before they tackle the change itself. Employees need to know what is expected of them and what support is available. They need to be able to express concerns in a public forum. In addition, they need to be allowed to think "outside of the box" in order to find workable solutions to tough problems.

Make it thy business to know thyself,

which is the most difficult lesson in the world.

~ Miguel de Cervantes

The process of shared accountability lies at the heart of change management. To put it a little differently, an "atmosphere" has to be created which allows managers to say "This is what I need from you and you and you," individually and collectively. Managing change means opening up dialogue, generating ideas and experimenting with different strategies and approaches.

It's a documented fact that at the end of World War II, when the Allies were bombing Berlin, there were still people in the Reichstag Chancellory finishing war reports that were due the next day—even with the knowledge that there wouldn't be a next day! Getting into fixed routines and assuming that change is something that is "out there" is not the way to succeed in business. There is a point at which being self-contained and rigid in how one operates becomes a kind of shield against possible change.

The shield also serves as a protective wall to hide the fact that behind the thought of change lies fear—something to be avoided at all costs, even if the price is the collapse of the business itself. Overcoming fear of change is not so much a process as it is a way of life. A leader must be able to play with change and teach others to play along with him. After a while, the game of change becomes not only commonplace, but challenging and enjoyable.

4. Leaders must lead with impeccable integrity.

"There comes a time when one must take a position that is neither safe, nor politic, nor popular, but he must take it because his conscience tells him it is right."

~ Martin Luther

To be a warrior is to learn to be genuine

in every moment of your life.

~ Chogyam Trungpa

George Orwell, the author of *1984*, was a corporal fighting on the Republican side in the Spanish Civil War. In one of his essays, he describes an incident at the front lines, facing the fascist army. Twelve soldiers were under his command. As part of their duties, the soldiers were ordered by Orwell to secure certain outlook positions. One soldier, whose position was exposed to enemy fire, refused the command. Orwell, after repeating the order several times, started dragging the man physically to his designated position. Instantly, the other men in his unit, all of whom were indigenous Spaniards, surrounded Orwell, telling him he was no better than the fascists.

The situation was becoming emotionally charged and personally threatening owing to the fact that Orwell's foreign status made him suspect. Suddenly, one of the soldiers, a dark skinned youth from a poor, lower-class family, leapt into the fray and made an impassioned speech defending Orwell, saying in his awkward dialect, *"No hay Cabo como el,"* which roughly translated means, "He's the best corporal we have."

The irony of this incident is that several days before, Orwell reported a box of cigars missing. He had stored them under his bunk. Prejudice being what it is, this same dark-skinned lad was accused by Orwell's superior officer of the crime. Subsequently, the poor lad was forced to undergo a humiliating strip search in front of Orwell and the other men. The soldier was, of course, totally innocent. Under normal circumstances, it would have been impossible for good feelings ever to be re-established between this young man and Orwell. But war has a way of changing conventional behavior, and this soldier realized, in his own naive, intuitive way, that Orwell was a man who possessed impeccable integrity—that his leadership arose from a vision of fairness and justice, a justice that transcended arbitrary judgments.

The young man was able to convey this feeling to his comrades in such a way as to justify Orwell's credibility as a leader worth following. This

Don't listen to friends when the friend

inside you says, "Do this."

~ Mahatma Gandhi

incident reveals two types of integrity: one, of a commanding officer, and the other, of his subordinate. Both men acted from a central core for what they believed to be right, regardless of the consequences.

Leading with integrity is not easy. It requires openness, courage and, above all, authenticity. Troubled businesses must have leaders with integrity if, for no other reason, that their environments are plagued by deception and selfishness. Acting from a position of truth increases the likelihood that leaders in dis-eased work places can build "critical masses" of like-minded followers. Leading with integrity exerts a positive force which functions as a powerful motivator for employees to exchange self-centered behaviors for ones that renew an organization's collective sense of purpose. Building a critical mass of support also helps create the kind of peer pressure that weakens the destructive power of "nay sayers" and would-be saboteurs.

In my experience, examples of impeccable integrity at mid and lower management are more common than at higher levels. The way you behave when no one is watching is a good yard stick for measuring personal integrity. Countless times, I've witnessed hard-working, dedicated line staff respond over and above the call of duty, often with little or no recognition from superiors. This is done from a sincere desire to be of help and make a difference. Individuals of this caliber believe that it's both right and proper to make sacrifices for the good of the organization. Their integrity, as expressed through constructive action, becomes synonymous with the goals of any forward moving enterprise—namely, to perform services that will help to integrate the operation as a whole.

By contrast, there are scores of managers who violate these principles. These are the types who instead of providing compassionate and frequently unsolicited service, hide in their offices or sneak out the back door before quitting time. These same individuals, however, are quick

Rest satisfied with doing well,

and leave others to talk of you

as they will.

~ Pythagoras

to write up employees for being a few minutes late or for taking a bit more time during a scheduled break. "Lapses" in personal integrity, such as the one described above, are almost always noted by the subordinate staff who are well-positioned to experience these behavioral double-standards first hand. Suffice it to say, after many of these slips in integrity take place, they add up to feelings that "management integrity" is nothing more than a gigantic oxymoron. When acting out of integrity becomes characteristic of an organization, dis-integration is never far behind.

It's no surprise that those managers whose actions reek with double standards are also quick to criticize employees who fail to respond to calls for increased productivity, better service delivery, improved communication or solid team work. The situation is only made worse in companies where double-standards are part of the organization's culture. In these circumstances, calls for improvement of any kind are usually met with cynicism and mistrust.

After listening to literally hundreds of pep talks from managers whose integrity is questionable, I often wonder if they are at all aware of how shallow they appear in the eyes of their subordinates. Managers who are out of integrity drain the company's health and vitality, much like blood-letting practices in the eighteenth century. As a result of this kind of behavior, many good people find that they have no alternative but to move on.

Embodying Your Highest Vision

There's a fine line between integrity and diplomacy. However, being in full integrity can produce transformational results, which makes the effort all the more worthwhile. I was once working with a city Department of Highways. One particular street crew in this depart-

Do not pray for easy lives, pray to be stronger men. Do not pray for tasks equal to your powers. Pray for powers equal to your tasks.

~ Phillips Brooks

ment had a reputation for being particularly hostile toward supervisors. There didn't appear to be any apparent solution, until, at my urging, the department placed a hard working, sincere young man from another service area in that dreaded supervisor spot. The initial reaction from most of the "old timers" on the crew was, "this guy's going to be eaten alive."

Like the Fleet Management case study discussed in Part One, this crew was poorly managed. Past history disclosed a string of authoritarian bosses with dubious levels of competence. This young man's style was in stark contrast to those of his predecessors. During the first couple of weeks he carefully observed how each man worked. He took copious notes. Evaluating the findings, he uncovered extensive inconsistencies. For example, the crew would never bring all of the proper equipment to the work site. When this happened, needless delays occurred, as work was halted until the needed piece of equipment was slowly transported to its designated location.

After making copies of the list of dysfunctions, he distributed them to all the crew members. Then, early one morning, he held a meeting. Going over all the points, without any finger pointing, he said, "Listen guys, I know YOU know these things I've listed are not the way to go about doing the job. I also know that you know a lot more about how to repair a street than I do. So here's what I'm suggesting ..... for this next project, let's all get together and decide how its going to be done, from start to finish. Whatever you decide, I'll go along with.

My job will be to support you in any way I can. What do you think?" At first, there was laughter and jokes about what they were going to do and how they were going to do it—all of which were geared toward not doing any work whatsoever. Then, some of the respected "old timers" spoke up. Their message was, "This young guy is offering us the chance to do things the right way for once, and he's not interested in looking

Is there anyone so wise as to learn by

the experience of others ?

~ Voltaire

over our shoulders or writing anybody up. Let's get behind him and show those x#xx@*^# in the City Manager's Office what we can really do!" With the support of the old timers, a critical mass of support arose. In short order, this crew became the most efficient, top-performing group in the department. The young supervisor got the results he wanted because he was interested in just that—results!

He didn't care about having to be the boss. He was perfectly willing to take on a supportive role. His integrity was revealed both in his awareness of the crew's dysfunctional behaviors, combined with his honesty in admitting that he really didn't know how to do the job as well as his crew. This young supervisor was doing his job according to his highest vision of what a city streets work crew was capable of doing—provided that everyone was pulling together in the same direction. His men understood that and were willing to abandon their unproductive habits to support the integrity of their supervisor. Very powerful stuff!

When your heart is in the right place, and you're able to demonstrate sincerity, honesty, dedication and openness, a sense of integrity emerges. This one characteristic alone yields a forceful leadership edge, especially when confronting the dis-eases inherent in dysfunctional companies.

Another illustration of how even the perception of integrity can exert a powerful force occurred during my first few weeks in the southwestern United States when I decided to apply for the position of "Tribal Administrator" at a Native American pueblo. Since I knew next to nothing about Indians, a friend suggested I read a short history of this particular tribe.

The book described a sacred lake and the appearance of an eagle dropping a feather on either side of the lake. This signified that the migrating band should divide into clans, one on each side of the lake. Armed with this information, I went to the interview. Several tribal

If our nature is permitted to guide our life,

we grow healthy, fruitful and happy.

~ Abraham Maslow

members were present, including two elders. The interview was going reasonably well, when quite unexpectedly one of the elders spoke up in his native language. One of the younger men translated his remarks: "He wants to know, who ARE you anyway, and why do you want to be involved with our people?"

Given the circumstances, I thought this was a great question. I thought for a moment, and replied, "When the eagle flew over the lake you can be sure of one thing: the name Barry Cooney wasn't pinned to either of the feathers he dropped."

There was a momentary silence while the young Indian translated my words. The two elders, after hearing the translation, paused, then exploded into uncontrollable laughter. Their response was so off-the-wall that everyone in the room started laughing. When things calmed down, there were a few more cursory remarks, after which I was promptly escorted to the door. Arriving home, I thought it highly unlikely that anything would come of this first encounter with these Native Americans.

Almost two weeks passed. Then, one morning, the phone rang. It was a pueblo representative calling. "You have the job," he exclaimed. I was dumbfounded. Why me? The conclusion I have drawn, based upon conversations with other Native Americans is that, in the eyes of the tribal elders, I was a man of integrity. I also appeared to possess some knowledge about their people, together with a dry humor that seemed to further indicate I was "OK."

Even though I was ignorant of tribal ways, they perceived me to be honest, bright, sensitive and curious—with no hidden agendas. These characteristics were, to them, the primary elements that mattered. These Ancient People placed a great deal of value on integrity. To them it signified wholeness and truth. And, after all, how can you sustain any management initiative without these things?

A man has to live with himself,

and he should see to it that

he always has good company.

~ Charles Evans Hughes

Managers who have lost integrity, or never had it to begin with, face an almost insurmountable battle to win the hearts and minds of their subordinates. Employees have memories like elephants, especially for actions that speak of double standards, betraying confidentiality, dishonesty or unfairness. These traits are not easily forgotten, particularly by people who have suffered as a result of them. Remember that managers are the standard-bearers for a company. Because of this, their attitudes and behaviors provide living examples of the values, attitudes and behaviors an enterprise calls its own. It only takes a few bad apples to "poison the well."

Integrity in a business needs to become not just a desirable characteristic, it needs to become an organizational way of life. How an organization handles both success and failure, how it shares information, how it attempts to resolve internal conflict, how it treats its internal and external customers, how it manages change and how it helps grow itself, all constitute moments of truth which determine the degree of integrity present.

Managers who aspire to become real leaders need to know that mediating integrity within their company is one of their most important responsibilities. There is no way to hide the results. They are revealed day in and day out to a constantly discerning group of employees and customers. Once again, I ask the reader to pause and think about the following questions:

Am I in full integrity?

Is my company in full integrity? If not, why not?

What steps must be taken to reach a point of maximum integrity?

Don't let the fear of striking out

hold you back.

~ Babe Ruth

5. Leaders must be prepared to take risks.

"..... and the time came when the risk it took
to remain in a tightly closed bud became
infinitely more painful than the risk it took to blossom."

~ Anais Nin

Whenever the topic of risk-taking arises, it's rare that you'll find anyone who doesn't have strong opinions. Those opinions are usually conditioned by personal experience and influenced by character and personality. Risk speaks of uncertainty, danger, potential harm or loss. Some people are notorious risk takers—even when the odds are against them; others are "wing walkers," who won't reach out for something new, different or potentially rewarding unless they're already holding on to something they perceive as solid.

In business, risk-taking is closely aligned with vision. Companies with limited vision are generally populated by low risk-taking people. Perhaps, at one time, while in a "start-up mode," many risks were attempted. However, once these enterprises became successful, the amount and degree of risk-taking behavior was drastically curtailed. Success has a way of lessening the desire to take risks. "After all," says the conventional wisdom, "if our ways of doing things have gotten us this far, why change?"

Sounds logical. But let's look at some facts: Less than fifty years ago, *FORTUNE* magazine published its first list of the five hundred biggest companies. By the early '90's only 29 of the top 100 firms could still be found in that top 100 ranking. And 25 years after that first

Statistically,

100% of the shots you don't take

don't go in.

~ Wayne Gretzsky

list was published, 230 of those 500 companies—46% of the entire "FORTUNE 500"—had vanished altogether! Clearly, the size of those companies and the enormity of their liquid capital still wasn't enough to insure survival.

A short time ago, the U.S. auto industry thought themselves invincible. They believed that energy would always be cheap and abundant, styling was more important than safety or quality engineering and foreign imports would never gain more than a few percentage points of domestic sales. Wrong! Wrong! And Wrong Again!! While these auto makers were thinking "invincible," the Arabs embargoed oil, Ralph Nader formed an army of safety-conscious citizens and the Japanese began perfecting "Zero Defect" production techniques.

Time marches on, and with each second more change takes place at an increasingly accelerating rate. Today, the average Joe on the street has more computing power in his wristwatch than existed on the planet before Kennedy was elected president.

The future, my friends, is not standing still. Proactive thinking and definitive action are the only paths worth taking. Resting on one's laurels is not the way to go. Because change is occurring with such rapidity, no organization is out of harm's way. Everything is now wrought with uncertainty. Today, the name of the change game bears strange resemblance to feeling at ease while suspended between two trapezes. Risk-taking is not only a fundamental part of playing this game, it's a fundamental part of the strategy for success. Leaders who find themselves in dis-eased companies must learn to feel more comfortable about risk. However, risk-taking needn't be carried on in isolation.

One thing that leaders must burn into their brain is "you have to do it yourself, but you can't do it alone." Ideas must be gathered from one end of the operation spectrum to the other. People from all areas of

Do not be too timid and squeamish about

your actions.   All life is an experiment.

~ Ralph Waldo Emerson

the workplace need to be involved in serious discussions about "who we are" and "where we are going." Brain-storming, together with constructing models of how things should look, must become part of a business' set of "S.O.P.'s"

Ways to generate constructive criticism must also be tested—especially in dis-eased companies, where misplaced criticism can lead to stonewalling and personal vendettas. Unless a dis-eased business can criticize itself openly and unashamedly, without sweeping its sensitive issues under the rug, it cannot hope to be restored to full health. In short, the doors need to be wide open for constructive criticism and new ideas, together with the willingness to take risks and deal with the consequences.

In the very act of doing this, risk-taking in and of itself becomes a synergistic process, a strengthened collective effort to solve problems and pursue common goals. This notion of pursuing common goals is the thread that ties everything together. The goals themselves need to be part of a greater vision.

No Vision is Realized Without Risk

My friend David lived in New York during the 1980's. In addition to being an accomplished musician, he also had a keen mind for business. In the midst of his musical activities, he noticed that Manhattan was filled with unemployed musicians. Further investigation revealed that many of these musicians were emigrés from the Soviet Union who had played with leading ensembles like the Moscow and Leningrad Symphony Orchestras.

What would it be like, David speculated, if these musicians could be gathered into one musical ensemble in greater Manhattan? The risks

Twenty years from now you will be more

disappointed by the things you didn't do

than by the ones you did. So throw off the

bowlines, sail away from the safe harbor,

explore, dream, discover ....

~ Anonymous

were formidable—after all, New York was one of the world's cultural capitals. It not only has dozens of musical ensembles, it plays host to countless numbers of national and international musical groups. Yet, the idea of taking artists who, because of their deep desire for political and religious freedom, left their country for a new land, and forming them into a splendid orchestra—this was a vision that could catch fire. This is what he felt. And so, out of this vision, the Soviet Emigré Orchestra was born.

In short order, a Board of Directors was formed, drawing people like Leonard Bernstein and Senator Jacob Javits. Soon concerts were booked in Carnegie Hall, Avery Fisher Hall at Lincoln Center and the Academy of Music in Philadelphia. At about the time that the Carnegie Hall concert was booked, it was my good fortune to step in as Co-Producer of this orchestra, at David's invitation. I saw first-hand how people from all walks of life were willing to work to see this vision of a musical ensemble of Russian emigrés become a reality. David himself invested heavily, using his own personal funds. Many others came forward to volunteer time and services.

I, myself, put my long-term career interests on hold to play a part in bringing life to this vision. Throughout this process a momentum was created, one which spoke of magic and possibility. When the right kind of energy is manifested, people will come together and extraordinary things will happen. The example of the creation of the Soviet Emigré Orchestra is not unique.

Whether in business or the arts, the challenge is always the same: to develop and continue to sculpt a solid vision, and then to have a toolbox filled with tools designed to assist in creating and sustaining that vision. *No vision is ever realized without risk. Yet, the synergy that arises from people believing in something has the effect of lowering the risk factor itself.*

Formulate and stamp indelibly on your mind

a mental picture of yourself succeeding.

Hold this picture tenaciously. Never permit

it to fade. Your mind will seek to

develop the picture.

~ Norman Vincent Peale

In dysfunctional companies, the risks that are undertaken are generally ones that, if successful, will bring life back into the enterprise. For example, the risks might involve rebuilding an entire work force or creating a new management team; it might entail restructuring the manner in which an organization delivers or sells goods; or, it might involve the complete dismantling of an inventory system or the consolidation of distribution centers. Whatever the risks, they represent more than just a band-aid alteration. In today's changing marketplace, risk-taking is commonplace. What isn't commonplace is doing it with a well thought-out strategy that allows people to buy-in with a collective sense of energy, enthusiasm and focus. For dis-eased operations, the costs of not taking risks are extremely high, given the fact that dysfunction is continuously erosive. To not take risks is to continue to spiral downward.

Nevertheless, just taking risks does not alone insure success. Leaders must make hard choices when it comes to deciding what kinds of risks will result in the greatest benefits. They, themselves, must be prepared to put their own jobs on the line to see that the risks they take come to fruition. It's the quality of self-sacrifice that distinguishes managers from true leaders.

When we factor in all the variables involved in risk-taking, we see that the majority of managers seem ill-equipped to sustain the effort and endure the sacrifices necessary for success. This is why risk-taking must be a fundamental training component for every individual groomed for a management position. Managers must become comfortable with the idea that risk-taking is not something that is only attempted by the foolhardy, that it need not be costly and that it offers the potential for bringing people together in powerful ways to address issues of common concern. In short, risk-taking must be used by leaders as a legitimate tool to spur growth, creativity and unity within an organization.

No man would listen to you talk if he didn't know that his turn was next.

~ Ed Howe

6. Leaders must learn how to listen.

"Women like silent men.
They think they are listening."

~ Marcel Ackard

Listening is not only a skill, it's an attitude. Talk to any divorce lawyer, marriage counselor or therapist. and you'll discover that one of the chief complaints they hear is "My husband (wife, boss, etc.) just doesn't listen." On a larger scale, dis-eased businesses are notorious for not listening to employees and customers—until they get a sharp message which says, "Goodbye, Charlie, I'm going somewhere else!" The inability to listen AND understand is one of the great weaknesses of managers and businesses in general. I'm of the opinion that most people hear only what they want to hear. Consciously or unconsciously, people merely go through the motions of listening. *Just being silent doesn't really mean you're listening. One has to listen with the intention of paying strict attention to what is being said.* If it sounds simple, it isn't. Considerable practice is required to be a good listener.

As a therapist in a large urban community mental health center, I once commented to a colleague, a psychiatric resident from South America, that I had a bad headache, the result of listening to patients for hours on end. He said he never had that problem. I asked him why. He turned his head, pointed to a hearing aid and said, "I just turn this off." Countless numbers of executives and managers turn off imaginary hearing aids every day and, in the process, miss out on vital information.

A manager who learns to listen enriches the jobs of his subordinates by giving them a sense of participation which helps both them and himself.

~ R.V. Araskog

Extensive research exists about the level of comprehension people have when listening. The results are consistently grim: It seems that most people don't understand half of what they hear—and shortly after they hear it, they forget half of that. Wait a day or two, and only 25% of the total amount of information given is retained. And all this is happening in a situation where people are supposedly paying attention! Imagine what retention there is if one is not interested in paying attention!

Have you ever been in a situation where you were talking with someone and their eyes were focused on everything but you? Have you experienced someone "listening" to you as they glanced anxiously at their watch? Or how about talking to a person whose non-verbal expressions clearly indicated that they were basically not interested in what you were saying? How do such "exchanges" make you feel? "Worth-less," I'll bet.

Not being heard is a big turn off. Everyone wants to think they're important enough to be listened to. In feudal times, it was customary for officials at all levels, up to the king himself, to grant audiences with the common folk. The purpose: to listen to their stories and acknowledge their complaints. The act of listening was, in this instance, both pragmatic and symbolic. Pragmatic in that it exposed real issues in the kingdom, province, town or village, and symbolic in that it demonstrated that even the poorest of the poor had a right to be heard.

There are plenty of reasons why people don't listen. Some individuals are easily distracted or chronically worried about other things. Others may not be interested in the subject matter at hand or they may find the information too complex to absorb. Others, still, might not like you or the way you communicate. I've observed that the majority of managers, when "listening" to others, seem to be thinking about what they're going to say next or constructing answers to questions, real or imagined.

Nature has given us one tongue, but two ears,

that we may hear from others

twice as much as we speak.

~ Epictetus

These are the self-centered managers. Those who seem to like to hear the sound of their own voice. In truth, they don't particularly care what any peer or subordinate has to say. This particular reason for not listening is an especially harmful form of dis-ease in the workplace. It clearly conveys a profound sense of disrespect. We all should be aware by now that if there is no respect among subordinates toward leadership, nothing of any importance can be accomplished. It is no surprise to learn that under-productivity is quite common in troubled businesses. Not listening to people is one of the underlying causes for this malaise. Idiomatically, this is known as "Communication Problems." What it really is, quite simply, is a failure to listen and respond appropriately.

Approaches to Effective Listening

There are many ways for leaders to listen effectively. I suggest to managers that they spend several hours each week engaged in conversations with people throughout the company ranks. I stress that these encounters should be more about listening and asking questions, with primary emphasis on the former. I advise them to always carry pocket note pads so that content can be written down immediately after the conversation takes place.

Periodic "climate surveys" are another way of listening to people. These surveys should be very simple, comprised of open-ended questions, to allow for all subjects to be brought up. Including one's name should be optional. However, it's often helpful to have some method for identifying what division, section, bureau or work group the surveyee is from—only because this helps to uncover common themes within smaller operating units. Once the data is in, it's important to share the findings with everyone. Otherwise, this form of "listening" will backfire.

The number one productivity problem in America is, quite simply, managers who are out of touch with their people and out of touch with their customers.

~ Tom Peters and Nancy Austin

In larger organizations, so-called "focus groups" comprised of small numbers of employees may be conducted to get a feel for what is on people's minds. There are legitimate concerns about this approach, however, regarding how open people are willing to be in the company of their peers or immediate supervisors. In this format, certain individuals will tend to monopolize discussions, leaving out employees who are quiet or passive by nature. Then, of course, there's the important issue of confidentiality, which must be guaranteed in order to have accurate feedback. My experience has led me to believe that all these formats—informal conversations, climate surveys and focus groups—should be utilized if a company is really serious about listening to its people.

Make no mistake about it, the nitty-gritty of listening is contained in one-on-one encounters. This is the format where the hearts and minds of followers are more likely to be won. The ability to open the mind, the heart and the ears will yield many converts to the leader's vision. Even if the leader disagrees with what is said, the act of truly listening enhances his image. It stamps him as someone who is attentive and empathetic, someone who deserves to be followed.

Time after time, after receiving intensive coaching about the importance of listening, executives will come back and say, "Wow, it's amazing what I learned," or, "After I thought about what I heard, I realized that these guys have a valid point." In fact, there are an infinite number of "valid points" that need to be uncovered in both healthy and dis-eased workplaces. Employing specific "listening strategies" will instill new life in any enterprise—even ones that appear to be quite fragmented. Listening creates an energy of appreciation and worth. Leaders who are able to convey these things to subordinates increase their stature in the eyes of those who are themselves enhanced.

I hadn't yet learned what I know now—

that the ability to communicate

is everything.

~ Lee Iacocca

Listening to customers is also the job of leaders. A common mistake is to have just one or two methods for getting close to the customer. There need to be as many as possible. Sending out questionnaires is one way that businesses try to listen to customers. This is OK, but more often than not, only customers that have very good or very bad things to say will fill out these forms. Another problem with this approach is that people have short memories and tend to emphasize certain things while ignoring others. Comment cards are also in vogue, but the same dynamics are at play here as they are with mailed questionnaires. Neither method should be relied upon extensively in determining what the customer is thinking.

One gaming corporation I was involved with was big on sending out surveys to guests. They judged the results by the number of "A" scores received. In my feedback to this company, aside from the fact that I always felt their numerical samples were too small, I also pointed out that people who lose sizable amounts of money gambling are hesitant to score his or her experience with a series of straight "A's."

Another variable here is the fact that in some people's minds, only God gets an "A." Furthermore, this guest service survey was actually damaging to the company because the results were linked to employee bonuses. Doing some informal number crunching of my own, the only consistent finding I could uncover was the following perplexing pattern: when the amount of "wins" in a casino rose, the guest satisfaction scores fell. Go figure! When I pointed out this inconsistency to several of the company's general managers, they merely nodded in agreement. However, none of them, by their own admission, would approach the corporate bosses with this information. They knew better. This company had the habit of shooting the messengers.

I'm told that Sam Walton, founder of Wal Mart, would make frequent trips to his stores throughout the country. When he did,

Nothing is interesting

if you're not interested.

~ Helen MacInnes

he was interested in finding out what the customers and employees were thinking. Leaders should never consider themselves too high up on the "org chart" to avoid getting into the trenches on a regular basis.

Sadly, many people in leadership positions only listen to numbers. In his book *Thus Spake Zarathustra,* the German philosopher Friedrich Nietzsche talks poetically about trees that grow so tall they can no longer see the smaller trees around them. This could serve as an apt metaphor for many top echelon corporate managers who don't pay much attention to anything save for increasing profitability—at whatever cost. This may, in part, explain why big business is so dis-ease prone. There are scores of CEO's who need to do much serious listening throughout their companies, if they are truly concerned about people as well as profit. Leaders in business must begin to realize that of all of the prophets there are that are worth listening to, few, if any, reside in corporate board rooms or executive suites.

7. Leaders must demonstrate compassion.

"I feel the capacity to care is the thing which gives
life its deepest significance and meaning."

~ Pablo Casals

The very idea of compassion in business strikes many as being somewhat sentimental, or, at the very least, incompatible with the notion of competitive markets and increased profitability. This concept is way off the mark. Compassion in business is first and foremost about values and principles.

One learns through the heart;

not the eyes or the intellect.

~ Mark Twain

With a sense of compassion, businesses—which, after all, are human enterprises—are obliged to ask questions such as: What are we about as a business entity? Are we primarily concerned with making money for ourselves and our shareholders, or are our concerns more expansive? What about the people who work for us—are they well compensated for their efforts? Are we, in any way, interested in sharing more of the wealth of our enterprise with them? What other needs might they have that, if provided, would make our work force even more focused on its mission? What interest do we have in supporting the communities that we live and work in? What does it mean to think globally and have a global consciousness?

Responding to these questions reveals nothing less than the soul of the organization itself. The recent scandals involving Enron, World Com, Tyco, Global Crossing, Adelphia and others have exposed a raw underbelly of greed and duplicity in our business communities. Many innocent, hard working people who believed in the integrity of these corporate monoliths have lost their life savings, and with it the opportunity to spend their final years in relative security. Of equal importance, these debacles have eroded people's trust and confidence in our free enterprise system itself, leaving the "common folk" to wonder if this free market system is merely a tool of the wealthy and powerful.

Without consumer faith our entire economic structure is threatened. While some social pundits and corporate CEO's have tried to downplay these events, the general public remains angry, nervous and skeptical. Any manager who wants to make a difference in their own life, and the life of their company, must begin to explore in earnest what "compassion-in-action" looks like. For business enterprises, compassion takes the form of expansive thinking about how to best serve people, providing assistance to those who do not have access to traditional means for achieving upward mobility, as well as an awareness that all of us are now part of a global community where the

The heart has its reasons that the mind

knows nothing of.

~ Blaise Pascal

impoverishment of some parts weakens the whole. Compassionate thinking recognizes that the battle for survival is, in many ways, the problem of mankind.

Expressed in a business context, compassion represents a certain kind of consciousness, a consciousness which supports creating more abundance for everyone. A compassionate perspective is one that acknowledges the hardships that many employees must endure to earn a living and support a family.

Despite increasing wealth, the polarization between rich and poor continues to widen. Unfortunately, many employees have discovered that while their expectations rise, their incomes remain flat. Rising expectations are part of the machinery of corporate capitalism which lures us to consume more and more products that aren't really necessary for survival.

As private debt increases, the pressure to consume remains constant, leading to internal conflicts which result in anxiety, depression and incidents of public and domestic violence. The ability to sort out priorities and think with clarity dissipates as people are driven to work longer hours to sustain lifestyles that are always just beyond their reach.

The workplace does not exist in isolation to this phenomena. In point of fact, the workplace is a microcosm of these values and experiences. Yet, at the same time, a huge schism exists between work life and private life. Unlike agrarian societies, where work life and home life are one and the same, our lives are fragmented, and within this fragmentation no attempt is made to bridge the gap between earning a living and just plain living.

Many children have no idea whatsoever of the nature of work or what kind of work their parents do for a living. Some time ago, there was

Be kind, for everyone you meet is fighting a hard battle.

~ Plato

was a television show featuring a host named Art Linkletter. One of the show's highlights were his interviews with young children. In one episode, Linkletter asked a little boy what his father did for a living. "He makes toilet paper and light bulbs," was the boy's reply. "Toilet paper and light bulbs? How do you know that?" Linkletter inquired. "Well," stated the boy, "That's what he always brings home in his lunch box." Obviously, the boy was distanced enough from his father's day-to-day work life that he had to grasp at whatever straws he could to understand what his dad did for a living. Such gaps in understanding can be eliminated by creating more transparent connections between home, work and community.

Compassionate thinking about the nature of work life and private life would greatly assist in making these connections more tangible and harmonious. The average working person is, on the whole, alienated in his place of work. He experiences no real sense of connection or meaning. There is only a sense of obligation. The predominant feeling is that one MUST work to live, and in the process, one must endure the alienation and fragmentation that the workplace engenders.

This state of affairs is even more acutely destructive in dis-eased companies, where just getting through the day can be a major accomplishment. Dis-eased companies, in particular, hunger for compassionate thinking. In such environments compassionate thinking means asking very basic questions: How much attention is placed on managing people consistently and fairly? How prepared is the business to think "outside the box" in addressing employee concerns? What kinds of programs or activities would demonstrate that the business really cares about helping to make people's lives qualitatively better?

All of this talk about compassion in dis-eased companies boils down to one fundamental question: What is it worth to have a loyal, dedicated, proactive work force? At this juncture, it's important to empha-

Compared to what we ought to be,

we are half awake.

~ William James

size that compassion does not equate with businesses acquiescing to abstract sets of worker demands. Rather, it speaks to the issue of the value placed on the individual. Stated somewhat differently, the kind of working environment that needs to be in place to foster solid accountability, innovative thinking and an ability to effectively deal with change, arises only from a more expansive concern for the worth of the individual. As organizations become larger and more successful, their relationship to individuals—employees, consumers, sub-contractors—becomes more complex. As this complexity increases, the underlying questions about the nature of compassion become more intertwined to include other cultures with differing economic conditions. For example, companies that employee or sub-contract child labor in foreign countries or purchase goods made by people in prisons face a whole other set of "compassion oriented" questions.

The Golden Law of Reciprocity

How leaders mediate "compassionate thinking" determines the degree of allegiance both employees and customers will extend to a business enterprise. Because of the nature of the technology of information, it's difficult for any entity, individual or collective, to keep many secrets. The manner in which a company conducts its business is now of particular interest to a more attentive and aware public-at-large. In fact, knowing how a company operates is just as important as the company's goods and services, in the eyes of many consumers.

There is now present in our society a real interest in knowing if the fancy footwear they buy is assembled by child labor for pennies a day, or if product defects, such as dangerous tires or excessively fatty hamburgers, are going to be adequately addressed. The public does, indeed, take notice when product manufacturing pollutes the air and endangers life. To believe otherwise is to deny the fact that

Never, my son, can a soul that has

so far uplifted itself as to grasp

the truly good and real, slip back

to the evil and unreal.

~ Hermes

consumers, in growing numbers, have reached a saturation point in their ability to tolerate deception, manipulation and exploitation. The intricate web of illusion that tries to separate products and services from processes and environments is now starting to unwind.

Apart from the altruism embodied in compassionate action, it is also an exceptionally good business strategy. That's because the "law of reciprocity," which supports a mutual interchange of responsibilities, is at work. Here's what I mean: Suppose you work for a company which appears to have your best interests in mind. Everyday, in some shape or form, it walks its talk. Because of these actions, the company has a legitimate right to ask for things in return—tangible things, like having its employees become fully responsible for carrying out their duties; to be dedicated team players; to collectively focus upon solving nagging operational issues; to maintain its commitment, as an organization, to develop cost-effective work practices and actively demonstrate flexibility in responding to change; to voluntarily take an active role in community affairs. Such enterprises would be perfectly justified in setting standards of this caliber for the people it hires.

This form of shared "response-ability" is guaranteed to produce energy, motivation, commitment and innovative thinking. By improving the quality of life of each employee, a business is essentially establishing a link between the need to work and the need for enhanced self-esteem. Examples of what this might look like include programs that seek employee involvement in decision making, planning, cost cutting or problem solving. Troubled businesses rarely involve their work forces in these kinds of undertakings. Instead, they are preoccupied with internal "war games" which determine who has power and who's in control. They are "egoistic" environments, in which alliances are formed only to maximize the probability that personal interests will be gratified.

Great works are performed not by strength

but by perseverance.

~ Samuel Johnson

If these conditions are to be eliminated, people must begin to look at the workplace with a new set of eyes. *By nurturing compassionate thinking, leaders are essentially bringing people together for the explicit purpose of renewing their sense of vigor, focus and involvement.* Compassionate thinking then becomes both a transformational tool and a philosophy. In these efforts, leaders need to make it a point to get closer to the work force, to understand workers' needs and desires. Taking this approach is basically an investment in the future, with the potential for enormous pay offs.

A colleague once told me about a *"maquiladora"* factory in Mexico which did electrical assembly for a large U.S. conglomerate. A fair-haired, fair-skinned guy from the Midwest was brought in as Plant Manager. What was different about this fellow was that he had a sincere interest in his workers and their culture.

Understanding the language, he set about exploring what the workers needs were. Medical care was a big concern. So were school books for their children, as well as decent clothes for them to wear. Responding to these needs, he purchased books and set up an in-house lending library. At the same time, he engaged the services of some local physicians who would then go directly to the worker's houses for diagnosis and treatment. He then managed to procure donations to buy children's clothes for the worker's families.

These gestures were not just a matter of good will. By his actions he demonstrated a core understanding of the value and importance that Mexican people place on the family. He was quietly yet firmly winning the hearts and minds of these workers. Sometime after these benefits were in place, the Plant Manager found himself in a terrible bind. Some "foul-up" at corporate headquarters had evidently resulted in a demand for many more "assembled pieces" than was humanly possible to produce, given the schedule of deadlines. What could he possibly do?

All things are possible until they are proved

impossible - and even the impossible

may be so as of now.

~ Pearl S. Buck

The Plant Manager decided to go directly to the workers and lay out the problem without any sugar coating. A meeting was called. After he spoke to the workers, several of the "informal leaders" asked if they could discuss the issue in private, without any directors present. "Yes," the Plant Manager replied, "this can be done." When the managers returned, the workers asked just one question: "Could our families come here and prepare us food, and bring bedding for us? "Of course," responded the Plant Manager. So they worked—day and night, around the clock, taking time only to get food and a little sleep. They worked until the order was filled. Reciprocal acts of compassion made this impossible task a reality.

You might think that this illustration could only take place in a developing country. However, there is no doubt that many readers of this narrative could provide personal examples about how caring and concern can motivate a work force to give service far in excess of what is expected. *So much of what experts call "effective leadership" is nothing more than focusing attention on bringing out the best qualities in people.*

Ironically, many acts of compassion are quite subtle. They don't require excessive amounts of time or expense, such as chatting with a janitor, sending a get well card to the ailing wife of an employee, helping someone muddle through some bureaucratic hoops linked to health benefits or what have you, having lunch on a regular basis with people who never get a chance to see or talk with you, asking people directly what they think about a policy or procedure, or better still, asking them to tell you honestly how they think you're doing and what you can do better.

Bear in mind that acts of compassion are acts of alignment. They come in all shapes and sizes. No matter what shape or size, the efforts have only one real purpose: to unify people in service to a common vision, and in the process, create a work entity that gives value to everyone.

Always bear in mind that your own resolution

to succeed is more important than any

other one thing.

~ Abraham Lincoln

8. Leaders must expand the concept of 'Reality' for those they lead.

"If you have built castles in the air, your work
need not be lost; that is where they should be.
Now put the foundations under them."

~ Henry David Thoreau

There's a story about a man strolling past a construction site. He sees three workers and asks each of them what they're doing. The first guy looks up and with a deep sigh, says "I'm laying bricks." The second fellow seems to be moving along with greater speed. When asked what he's doing, he answers, "I'm putting up a wall." The third individual seems not only to be moving along smoothly with his work, but with great care—his work is flowing and he appears to be in great spirits. When asked the same question, he looks up and proudly says, "I'm building a cathedral."

All three men were doing the same work. To one, it was pure drudgery; to the other, it was just another day's work; but to the third, it was a magnificent undertaking, performed with focus and commitment. It would be any business' good fortune to have an entire work force reflect the attitudes and behaviors of the last worker.

However, just wishing for excellent performers isn't enough to make it so. Leaders must be catalysts for creating more expansive perceptions of what the "reality" of one's work is all about. Making this happen is a two-step process. First, the employee needs to understand the connection that his job has with every other job. This is best done

Life is not measured

by the number of breaths we take,

but by the moments that take

our breath away.

~ George Carlin

experientially. The effective leader will make sure that, over time, every employee has the opportunity to find out what it's like to be in someone else's shoes. Offering these experiences when an employee is first hired is a good start; however, they need to be revisited periodically—perhaps on a semi-annual basis.

Fostering a thorough understanding of an organization is the best way to explain why exceptional communication between different parts of the operation is mandatory. For example, the simple act of showing hotel housekeepers front desk operations insures a deeper understanding of the importance for housekeepers to inform the front desk that rooms are clean and ready for occupancy. By observing and learning the in's and out's of front desk interfaces with hotel employees and guests, housekeepers can begin to internalize what it means to provide timely information. In the process, they also are able to observe, first hand, how communication bottlenecks develop.

Let me cite another illustration, this one in an accounting department. Few people who don't crunch numbers for a living are especially interested in accounting. All they generally want is to be handed their checks on time. As such, it is not typically understood what kind of information payroll operations or accountants need to do their jobs, not to mention the complexities of reading a detailed budget. The accounting department I'm referring to took the time to explain to people in other departments the complexity of their work, and along with it, how budgets are determined. All this was done in order to share information with employees about internal expenses and the workings of an intricate internal budget.

The results were startling! Employees suddenly had a different view of their company as they poured over operational expenses and "hidden" operating costs. (It was amazing to see the expressions

I arise in the morning torn between

a desire to improve the world

and a desire to enjoy the world.

This makes it hard to plan the day.

~ E.B. White

on workers' faces when they discover how much the company paid out for overtime and how expensive it was to keep the lights on.) Sharing this accounting information expanded the reality of these workers. They, in turn, developed a more caring approach about waste and excessive consumption.

Developing insights about various aspects of a business expands a person's ability to understand complexity and appreciate the fact that they are only part of a much bigger picture. When this understanding is firmly implanted, it becomes easier to understand why every point of contact by one segment of the operation with another offers opportunities to add value to a company's overall performance.

Troubled companies see these points of contact in very simplistic ways. Everything appears to be tied to someone's personal agenda. Stepping outside that narrow perspective provides the first step in learning about the nature of strategic thinking. When everyone is properly aligned in their roles and relationships, a positive flow is felt throughout the entire organization. This insight only comes about through exposure. People need to be shown how different parts of the organization align with other parts. They can't do this by memo!

The second part of the process of expanding employees' reality involves creating and sustaining a "vision" of how things should look. Basically, any vision contains many smaller ones. For example, the vision of maximizing efficiency throughout the workplace can be broken down into a series of smaller visions about efficiency within and between operational units. The smaller visions always act in support of the larger one. In other words, the smaller or "secondary visions" spell out all the "how to do it's." More will be said about this process when the concept of "Strategic Partnering" is discussed in Part III.

If you think you're too small to be effective,

you've never been in bed with a mosquito.

~ Anonymous

<u>The Rewards of Inclusion</u>

Visions are always works-in-progress, subject to change and modification. In successful businesses, nothing remains static. The exact opposite is true for dis-eased operations, where most activities appear inert or "out of focus." One of the big success stories I can recall involved a former city government client, specifically, a water and sewer crew. When I first encountered this outfit, they had a poor self-image in relation to other city crews. Colleagues in other departments were always berating these workers as being laggards who were always "up to their ears in shit," (literally and figuratively). They were right—this crew was totally dysfunctional. Personal conflicts and operational confusion were the operative norm. I quickly surmised that considerable time needed to be spent with the supervisor of this outfit. He was an "old hand at water work," as he liked to say, knowledgeable, with a pleasant disposition.

Because he was soon to be retired, his interest in putting together a first class team was half-hearted at best. I spoke with him about expanding his crew's concept of what their jobs were all about. At first, he wasn't quite sure what I meant. Finally, he got it: For everything to work flawlessly, each person had to be attuned to what the other was doing; everyone had to depend on each other to provide the right information and perform the right task at the right time.

In addition to job interface, we also discussed the importance of each person's duties, as well as the sacrifices that each man made in order to bring service to the community in times of crisis, such as when a water main ruptured in the middle of the night.

He admitted that not enough of this kind of talk took place. I then explained what creating a vision of "service excellence" was all about, and how each person was a vital contributor to that process. I could

Man will only become better when you make him see what he is like.

~ Anton Chekov

see that for the first time in a long time he felt some excitement. The more I talked with him, the more he seemed to recall instances when he actually did have a vision of what a top-notch water and sewer crew looked like. But years of what he termed "bureaucratic B.S." had made him cynical and lethargic. It wasn't that his crew was so bad, he stated, it was that the "guys above him" had worn him down. They were the cause of his discouragement.

After more detailed coaching, a series of meetings were held—each one short, sweet and to the point. His crew started to sense their boss's renewed energy and concern. Soon his energy became infectious. The crew members became sincerely interested in learning more about each other's jobs. They took particular interest in the work done by a fellow who sat in a truck looking at a monitor that received images from a special camera sent into a sewer line to detect blockages or structural defects. Prior to these meetings, he was widely ridiculed for watching "dirty movies" all day. (Truth be told, this fellow really liked his job and would talk endlessly about all the strange items that could be detected floating around in the sewer!)

By the time this "visioning process" was rolled out, the group was noticeably more aligned. They started to realize the importance of their jobs, both in relation to one another and in relation to the entire community. The repair crew's solidarity was quickly tested one day when a major sewer line burst. Coordination with local police was necessary, as was contact with a local school, which was located near the broken line. The supervisor himself had grown in stature in the eyes of his men and he responded, in kind, with targeted "on purpose" leadership.

In this brief case study, a number of organizational issues were addressed: First, a disempowered supervisor became an effective leader; second, the crew's morale was lifted; third, a deeper under-

Man's mind once stretched by a new idea

never regains its original dimensions.

~ Oliver Wendell Holmes

standing of the interconnection of everyone's job was made part of the crew's mind-set; and lastly, a vision of performance excellence was developed and put into place. If any one of these issues had not been effectively handled, the crew would not have been able to achieve its high level of success.

So often, interventions with groups are not well thought out. If the person in charge has limited leadership capabilities, the end result will be flawed. Likewise, if a proper relationship between people's roles and responsibilities isn't made clear, the outcome will suffer. Finally, if a clear vision isn't in place, the group effort will not be able to sustain itself. Just getting "some ducks in a row" will not produce the "quacking" that's needed. Your operation might quack like a duck, but unless all of these items are present, you might end up with a limping goose instead of a healthy duck.

When this project first began, I intuited that the water department's supervisor had what it took to be an effective leader. But he, himself, had to first buy into that vision. Once effective interventions are put into place, they need to be continually reinforced. If, for example, the entire city government initiated a similar intervention program on a larger scale, the forward moving energy may have been enough to sustain this weak department, in spite of its less-than-inspired leader.

However, this particular city government was a huge pocket of disease. As a result, the water department couldn't rely on the larger organizational superstructure for support. They had to do it themselves and keep moving on their own steam. That kind of effort becomes hard work when there's no assistance from the top managerial echelons. Nevertheless, this, like many other work groups, needed its leaders to expand their understanding of the importance of mutual interdependence. In addition, they needed to formulate a

Use what talent you possess: the woods

would be very silent if no birds sang

except those that sang best.

~ Henry Van Dyke

concise picture of what an ideal water and sewer crew looked like, clearly spelling out the attitudes and behaviors required to build a high performance operation.

The importance of managing according to a solid vision cannot be understated. When a clear vision is in place, all actions, plans and decisions are pointed in that direction. This act of measuring all actions in terms of how they contribute to the realization of a company vision is called "alignment."

It's important for managers to not assume that alignment is clearly understood by everyone. Because of this, certain questions must be asked once a vision appears to be in place. One key question is: How aligned are our actions in relation to our stated vision? Similarly, when coaching or correcting staff members, the same question must be asked, albeit in a slightly altered fashion: Is what I'm requesting of this person in alignment with our vision?

Allowing all operational, policy and procedural issues to be measured against a company's vision is a valid litmus test for determining the extent to which an organization is internally walking its talk. When different sectors of the business are acting, thinking or planning at cross purposes, it's obvious that things are not in proper focus. Alignment is the process that allows "hand and glove" relationships in pursuit of a common vision to manifest. If no clear vision exists, then any attempt at alignment will be off the mark.

Companies whose managers are not comfortable or skilled at asking questions and determining how aligned their operation is, are setting the stage for dysfunctional processes to emerge, or, if already present, to mushroom out of control. That's because when activities are mis-aligned, communication and procedural duties become disconnected.

Better to light one small candle

than curse the darkness.

~ Chinese Proverb

Consequently, a fundamental characteristic of dis-eased organizations is internal disconnectedness. For example, if you go into any company and spend time listening to people in meetings, you'll quickly get a sense of dysfunction based on the degree to which people appear to be talking past one other—or alternatively, by taking note of how many issues remain unresolved or only partially attended to.

When organizations of this type come to a fork in the road, you can be sure they'll take it! As the saying goes, "if you haven't a clear direction, any one will do." Having sets of interlocking visions that fit easily into a larger collective vision means that the organization is fully aligned. Once "vision" and "alignment" become part of a business's mind-set, it can more readily calibrate its thinking and actions when it begins to stray off the path.

Developing workable visions within a company is challenging, as is cultivating a collective mind-set which understands the relationship between a vision and the attitudes and behaviors which need to be in place to make that vision become reality. Without a clear set of visions and proper alignment of corresponding attitudes and behaviors, companies often find themselves in a constant "fire-fighting" mode. After a while, fire-fighting becomes a business-as-usual activity. At some point, the fires start to join one another and the whole operation finds itself ablaze.

Things are moving incredibly fast nowadays, so much so that developing strategies and executing them with lightning precision is the only sure way to remain competitive. Not unexpectedly, the responsibility for moving forward falls squarely on the shoulders of the leader whose job it is to see that understandable visions become a fundamental part of every employee's mind set. In the final analysis, it is this kind of strategy that will result in successful outcomes.

If at first you don't succeed ....

you're running about average.

~ M.H. Alderson

9. Leaders must take action.

"You can't build a reputation on what
you're GOING to do."

~ Henry Ford

As a graduate student, I was politically active. This was in the 1960's and early 1970's, when people were being drafted "en masse" to fight in Viet Nam. At the time, we "activists" were critical of the so-called "Establishment." Characteristic of this activism were endless internal debates addressing the merits of this or that kind of social order.

These debates would continue into the wee hours of the night—night, after night, after night. I often found myself mentally and physically exhausted after a string of these mental marathons. Nothing ever was resolved. Even planning a simple protest demonstration would take days, only to fizzle out at the last moment because no consensus could be reached. I left graduate school feeling completely fed up with political activism, which seemed to me a conflict of terms. Instead, I wanted to really DO things.

Years later, venturing into one dis-eased company after another, I experienced similar unfolding dynamics—talking and planning, talking and planning—but never any action. Being an active part of these environments was exhausting. At first, I couldn't understand how anyone in their right mind could tolerate such stifling environments. Gradually, I began to understand. Non-action was a convenient way of avoiding responsibility.

Be bold—and mighty forces will

come to your aid.

~ Basil King

Failure to act is worse than taking action and failing. Failed actions are great instructional tools. Troubled companies fail to act in many ways: They don't effectively address internal issues which impede performance; they wait and wait until situations get so out of control that drastic rescue actions must be taken, often with unpredictable results; communication in every direction is sluggish—important information is either not properly assimilated, not made available, or both. These tendencies serve to increase the probability that bad decisions or no decisions will become the norm.

There is a myth about dis-eased businesses that they are ready to collapse. This isn't necessarily the case. Most troubled businesses are merely mediocre in the extreme. Their demise is incremental and often undetectable for quite some time. The reason for this mediocrity is that they just can't get themselves out of first gear. They have poor "response-ability." This characteristic is closely linked to the organization's culture, which supports the notion of moving slowly and carefully—that is, too slowly and too care-fully—to remain competitive.

Operations that exhibit these characteristics try very hard to protect themselves from failure; but in the end, they only induce it. These businesses typically come from the "Old School" where predictability and control reign supreme. Given the lack of strategic alignment which is so characteristic of these outfits, their operations degenerate into ones that become quite unpredictable and out of control—the very opposite of what they so desperately want and need.

When you ask representatives of these kinds of companies to talk about what makes them stand out from the rest of their industry, one usually receives a "deer in the headlights" stare. By contrast, businesses that are comfortable taking action are those that have leaders who not only don't mind the risks involved, they are excited about

Just do it.

~ advertisement for running shoes

the possible outcomes. "Let's find out what happens if we try this," would not be an unusual remark from an action-oriented leader.

When faced with internal processes that aren't working, the action-type leader becomes restless, while the manager who seeks predictability searches for sequential solutions, which, more times than not, are a disguise for band-aid approaches to existing challenges. Getting out of a "predictability" mind-set can be like chiseling through granite. There are times when managers from the "predictability school" find it impossible to become action leaders. They are either too cautious, too frightened or too narrow in their thinking to make the leap. At this stage, managers of this ilk are nothing more than "dead weight."

Given the many bad habits that are pervasive in most businesses, chances are reasonably good that many competitors are in equally bad shape. But ignorance is bliss—and so it is that many organizations with dis-eased operating habits feel completely at ease in their own discomfort. They believe they are inching forward, but this thinking is purely illusional.

It may seem obvious, but taking action can be a form of innovation, especially in organizations whose cultures are, by custom and habit, slow moving. Taking action speeds things up, forcing one to think on one's feet. One of the ways to take action is to assess the merits of this or that and, in so doing, get everybody involved—customers, vendors and employees alike.

There's nothing wrong with saying, "Look, we're interested in trying this out. We want to be on the cutting edge of things, and we're not afraid of making mistakes. But we need your sincere buy-in, and we need your input. Tell us everything you think that might work or not work about this action or endeavor." By opening innovative pro-

He who hesitates is poor.

~ Zero Mostel
(Line from "The Producers")

cesses to collective scrutiny, a company is creating both interest and energy. The message that's being delivered is strong and clear: "We value your input. Let's really put this thing under the microscope as a work-in-progress. If it needs fine-tuning—great, we'll do it. If it proves to be something that doesn't work, we'll scrap it. But let's all get in there and see how it serves us. It's all of our responsibilities to try this out, and see if it works."

There are a few important implications in sending out a message like this. First, in the act of rolling out something new and having everyone provide input, the leader is reinforcing the concept of enhancing an employee's sense of being valued—which is the basic underlying axiom for counter-acting organizational dis-ease.

Second, whatever the innovation is, it becomes a shared part of the collective experience—which means that people are much more invested in the outcome. This means they are less prone to blaming others. In other words, by attempting innovation, an enterprise has the opportunity to make this action a shared "response-ability."

Third, by taking action, and "leaping" rather than attempting to analyze and over plan, the business is shaping a new company culture. This culture is one that is learning to be excited about change and innovative thinking. It's a culture that recognizes and accepts the possibility of failure, devoid of negative associations.

By attempting innovation, the culture begins to see itself as being truly innovative, proactive and forward moving. This type of energy, in turn, attracts people who are characteristically innovative and forward moving. Lastly, by opening these processes to collective scrutiny, a company is able to look at performance and participation with a new set of eyes. This new "vision" enhances the likelihood that new leaders will emerge to assist in the recruitment of a more committed

Have no fear of perfection—

you'll never reach it.

~ Salvador Dali

group of followers. In this action framework, the business becomes sharper in its ability to identify those who are making worthwhile contributions versus those who are just along for the ride.

Lessons from the Competition

Innovations that are developed in the executive suites at corporate headquarters and then templated onto field operations have a less than even chance of succeeding. This is because, more times than not, there exist huge gaps in communication between corporate and field offices. It appears that the underlying causes for such disconnects are based on myopic obsessions of who's in charge. "Corporate" thinks it knows what's best; the field operations think that corporate does not fully comprehend "field conditions"—nor do they even care to.

A regional sales representative for a leading copying company told me about how hard it was to deal with her corporate office and how little understanding they had about conditions in the field. She related an instance where a long-term client, one that generated a considerable amount of business for the company, was experiencing difficulty getting adequate servicing of their copying machines.

A rival firm was proposing a seemingly better, more innovative package with a product that had been getting many kudos for its quality and durability. The client asked for a slight discount in its fees to continue using this sales rep's product. When she explained the situation to the "boys at corporate" she was told that "under no circumstances would the company lower its fees—period." Our sales rep lost the client. However, what was lost was more than a client. It was the opportunity to find out what wasn't working and what the rival firm had to offer that was so attractive.

If you're going to do something wrong,

at least enjoy it.

~ Leo Rosten

Bending over backwards to retain loyal customers and discover what they want and need should be the order of business for any company that wants to stay ahead. In the above example, corporate policy, dictated from afar, was responsible for not just losing the client, but not using the situation to learn more about the competition. Surely, if this loyal customer was drawn away, what about customers who are not especially loyal to the firm in question?

Companies can often learn about innovation from their competitors, and then do it better. Following the end of World War II, Japan was known for making toys and transistor radios. In those days, when you thought about Japanese products, the words that came to mind were "copy," "cheap," "imitation," "poor quality." But Asians have shown themselves to be were quick learners. Before very long their electronic and automotive technology was dominating world markets. It took North America years to regain a reasonable market share. What were we doing all this time, here in the U.S.A.? The answer is, "not paying attention."

To be an "Action Leader" requires you to pay attention. A loss of a sale or a valued customer is cause for critical concern. That concern should not be just reflective. The Action Leader must emphasize that everything needs to be continually evaluated and scrutinized. That's why it's so important for leaders to destroy turfs wherever they exist. The very existence of turfs suggests that things are not being properly scrutinized. As you may recall, it's the job of a turf to protect itself from scrutiny. Taking action and being proactive can be maximally effective only if the organization is flowing—meaning that its members are performing with a sense of mutual cooperation and openness.

In my brief stint as a state government Department of Health executive, I was particularly critical of the Legal Division. It seemed that the state lawyers wanted to be involved in everything. They acted in such a way as to create the impression that everything was subject

Don't play for safety - it's the most

dangerous thing in the world.

~ Hugh Walpole

to litigation. They fostered a kind of in-house paranoia, manifesting the perception that at any given moment, some disgruntled employee would sue the department.

If a contentious issue arose involving a manager and a line staff employee, the lawyers insisted on setting up barriers which prevented one party from having a constructive, mediated discussion with the other. I had the distinct impression that every internal personnel issue the lawyers touched turned to manure.

Because of my position as Deputy Assistant to the Department Secretary, I was able to hold these lawyers at bay—most of the time. It wasn't easy. I received no cooperation whatsoever from my boss. He was a man of inaction, whose primary purpose was to maintain the status quo and avoid any appearance of being the head of an "untidy" house.

Given how much internal chaos resulted whenever the lawyers were involved, I pleaded with the Secretary himself for assistance. His response was always one of benign neglect. Toward the end of my tenure, when my "aggressive" stance toward departmental dysfunction placed me out of favor with the powers that be, my office was relocated to a small closet-like space—in the Legal Division—a fate equivalent to a devout Muslim having his heart cut out and wrapped in a pig's skin. This relocation was a signal that my departure from state government was imminent.

I wondered, at the time, whether non-governmental, "for profit" businesses would tolerate one part of the organization to cause such disruption to the other parts. Wouldn't someone in charge take action when they saw this happening? Much to my chagrin, these kinds of goings-on would become everyday occurrences once I immersed myself into assisting dis-eased "for profit" companies.

We find the defendants incredibly guilty.

~ (Trial scene in Mel Brook's film
"The Producers")

Many managers, particularly those in top positions, continually refuse to take action when they see one part of the business at odds with another. They are under the impression that things will work themselves out on their own. Sometimes this is the case. Apparently, these people fail to understand that there's no time to waste when sluggishness or incongruent behavior is uncovered.

Any leader worth her salt will not be afraid to take action to eliminate patterns of non-cooperation, ignor-ance, or poor communication between different parts of the operation. There are instances when managers will fail to act because they want to please everyone. Individuals of this type are under the false impression that if people are pleased (or appeased?) with how they are treated, they will naturally be inclined to act in the best interests of the company. We need to dismiss this notion immediately.

If you try to please everyone, ...

There are very intelligent, politically savvy individuals (some of whom you may know by name), who will consistently act to enhance their own positions of authority, whether or not it helps or hinders company operations. Action Leaders are not beauty contest contenders. They don't need to be liked. They need to be respected and listened to. Putting forth clear guidelines which support mutual cooperation, in the full sense of the term, and making sure these guidelines are adhered to by everyone—this is the mark of an Action Leader. Anything less jeopardizes the integrity of the operation and exposes it to the kind of favoritism that breeds virulent organizational dis-ease.

Taking action doesn't necessarily mean chopping off heads. However, people who clash with one another, or whose actions disrupt more than contribute, must be read the "Riot Act." Dialogue is the key to

I've got to keep breathing.

It'll be my worst business mistake if I don't.

~ Sir Nathan Meyer Rothschild

understanding. If people can't work things out successfully in short order, they quickly become a burden to the operation.

A manager in a leading gaming company I worked with always tried to please everyone. Without question, he was a sweet guy, gregarious and knowledgeable. Everyone liked him—and everyone walked all over him. Talking with him informally, I asked him what his childhood was like. Apparently, he grew up in a very large southern family. He was one of ten children. In his household everyone had to get along with everyone else. That was the price of survival. He brought this philosophy with him into the workplace. It proved to be his undoing.

There is a parable which drives this point home: It concerns a boy, a man and a donkey. The boy rode on the donkey and the old man walked alongside. As they continued to walk, they passed a group of people who remarked, "It's such a shame that the old man must walk, while the young boy rides." The old man and the boy thought perhaps the critics were right, so they changed places. Later, they passed more people, and took note when they remarked, "What a shame that man makes that little boy walk." So both the man and the boy decided to walk. Sometime later, they passed more people, who laughed and commented about how stupid it was for the man and boy to walk when they had a decent donkey to ride. So they both hopped on the donkey's back and continued their journey. Soon they passed more people, who were quite vocal about the fact that the boy and the man were putting such a heavy load on a poor donkey. Both the boy and man thought they might be right. They promptly got off the donkey, picked him up and started carrying him. When they attempted to cross a narrow wooden bridge, they lost their grip, and the donkey fell into the river and drowned.

The management lesson which needs to be understood: "If you try to please everyone, you'll eventually lose your ass." Action Leaders

The road to hell is paved with good intentions;

The road to heaven is paved with good deeds.

~ Anonymous

can't afford to please everyone. That's why it's necessary for anyone who assumes a leadership position to gain more understanding about their leadership style, and the effect that such a style has on sustaining buy-in and keeping performance and motivation high.

In the absence of targeted training and coaching, many managers form their management styles based upon developmental experiences in childhood. If your dad "kicked you in the butt" and told you to do this or that, chances are good that you employ this same tactic, with a few minor variations, when directing subordinates. Action Leaders don't act just for the sake of acting. They have a plan, they understand the parts that each person or group segment must play in that plan, they set about to get others to buy in to that plan and they promote synergism to see that that plan is carried out. Along the way, things get evaluated and input is received from all directions.

The leader then takes all the available data and, in conjunction with others, makes whatever modifications are needed. Every action that is initiated should have a "strategic" purpose—one that is in full alignment with the greater vision of the entire enterprise.

Being identified as an Action Leader can bring immediate health to an ailing business. The reasons for this are as follows: Being an Action Leader implies that important issues will not be swept under the rug, that no favoritism will be shown, that people will be held accountable, that a game plan will be in place, that change and risk-taking are factors which the game plan has taken into account and that people will be rewarded according to their value and contributions to the organization, as they work to see that plan come to fruition.

That may be a considerable amount of medicine for a sick business to swallow all at once, and the taste may not be the most appealing at first. Nonetheless, dis-eased organizations must often

People seem not to see that their opinion

of the world is also a confession of character.

~ Ralph Waldo Emerson

be shocked out of their malaise if they are to survive. Those who have the constitution to tolerate the treatment will lend added strength to the operation; those who succumb would have done so regardless of the circumstances. An Action Leader understands that a critical mass of like-minded, same-spirited people must be present to manifest a successful turnaround. Yet again, the axiom for successful change surfaces: "You have to do it yourself ...... but you can't do it alone."

10. Leaders must develop people.

"It is one of the most beautiful compensations of life that no man can sincerely try to help another without helping himself."

~ Ralph Waldo Emerson

Leaders cannot hope to achieve their goals without engaging the help of others. Results oriented managers are good at formulating strategies and telling people what to do. Leadership, however, embodies more expansive connections with potential followers.

It is possible for someone to carry out a leadership role alone. But that kind of stance can become exhausting and isn't terribly productive. Leading alone poses still other limitations. You can't be everywhere directing everything at once, nor can you hope to sustain a vision, reinforce it and clarify it all by yourself. Given the broad array of tasks involved in leadership, it makes good sense to empower others to assist in directing, planning and motivating others. Being a leader in a dis-eased business poses unique challenges that are far in excess of those in companies that are performing well.

Drive thy business or it will drive thee.

~ Benjamin Franklin

Troubled businesses are filled with discontented people who feel severely disempowered. It therefore becomes imperative to grow people internally. So much of the malaise that overtakes a dis-eased business has roots in employees feeling constrained, micro-managed and devalued. Providing leadership opportunities is a tried and true mechanism to remove impediments and bring new life to a morally depleted work force.

Many of the leadership principles I've introduced contain the seeds for developing people. For example, having a strong determination to lead encourages others to feel a similar kind of resolve. Likewise, uplifting people with positive attitudes enables them to think more optimistically, producing even more synergistic energy.

Also, helping people move through fear is a way of removing deep-seated blocks which inhibit employees, preventing them from being the very best they can be. Once certain fear-based barriers are eliminated, leadership ability can be quickly identified. The irradication of fear-based inhibitions has a transformative effect, one which has been eloquently captured by Guillaume Apollinaire:

> *"Come to the edge," he said.*
> *They said, "We are afraid."*
> *"Come to the edge," he said.*
> *They came.*
> *He pushed them....*
> *And they flew.*

In a similar vein, by leading with integrity, the leader is modeling values he believes should be reinforced. Followers pick up on this dynamic, realizing that the leader is setting a benchmark for the way employees and customers need to be treated. Another important leadership task is to demonstrate what it means to take measured risks and calculate

If someone says "can't"

that shows you what to do.

~ John Cage

the gains which might result, as well as weighing the consequences that must be borne, if the risk-taking initiative fails.

Developing people requires observation, modeling and coaching. Not everyone can get this special treatment from a leader. It's important to grasp the fact that leadership development is a process that is constantly expanding outward; that is, the leader mentors people who, in turn, are committed to mentoring others. When this process is in full swing, there's no reason why every employee can't carry out some form of leadership activity, regardless of size or scope.

I recall an incident which involved a middle-aged man who worked on the maintenance crew of a former manufacturing client. Among other things, the plant manager was concerned about the quality of maintenance at the facility, due to a noticeable drop in performance quality in the preceding year. One day, I received a short memo: Would I look into it, and see what I could come up with?

The man I wanted to involve was not well educated. Though after talking with him several times, I could sense he had a lion's share of street smarts. He was a hard working, quiet sort of guy, unassuming and well mannered. In our conversations, he seemed very interested in the management development projects I was spearheading for his company. I approached him about the possibility of helping me put together a brief questionnaire for his colleagues in Maintenance— questions which would help determine some possible causes for this outfit's less than stellar work performance over the last year.

I wish I had a camera handy to photograph the expression on this man's face when I asked if he would like to help me. His eyes lit up like a Christmas Tree! No one had ever requested him to do anything other than his normal duties. During the following week, I met with him twice, at short intervals. At our first meeting, he presented me

During my eighty-seven years

I have witnessed a whole succession

of technological revolutions. But none of

them has done away with

the need for character in the individual

or the ability to think.

~ Bernard M. Baruch

with a number of issues he thought might be appropriate. Although his write-up of questions was rife with misspellings and awkward grammar, he managed to come up with a handful of items that, based on his knowledge of maintenance operations, were worthwhile contributions. I mentioned to his supervisor the good work he had done. At my suggestion, the supervisor promptly wrote a letter of commendation and placed a copy of it in the man's personnel file.

Not long afterward I learned that this once reclusive maintenance worker was now volunteering for all sorts of committees and in-house activities. He had taken the "empowerment ball" and ran with it. Some months later, I ran into his supervisor in the employee dining room. He related the changes that had taken place with this gentleman. "He's a different person since he helped you with that survey," I was told. The supervisor went on to describe how the fellow was now providing input on a regular basis. The supervisor concluded by saying, "You know, I'm considering making this guy one of our Leads."

This small but significant incident provides a fine example of what can happen when someone is given a little attention, some empowerment and a bit of recognition. There are so many employees in our labor force who are capable of making outstanding contributions, if only given the opportunity.

Enhancing Management Bench Strength

In any discussion about techniques for growing people, the leadership concept of "listening to others" needs to be right at the top of the list. In the act of listening and paying attention to the other, the sense of self worth is greatly enhanced. This is true for not just the

I'm a great believer in luck, and I find that the harder I work the more I have of it.

~ Thomas Jefferson

so-called "lower level" jobs. Everyone in an organization can benefit from the self esteem that arises when a leader devotes time to really listening to what others around him are saying.

When subordinates recognize that leaders are listening, there is a certain openness which springs forth—an openness that results in a desire to share ideas and opinions, without reservation. These kinds of occurrences are breaths of fresh air within companies whose employees feel that their input isn't wanted.

Not only does listening serve as an excellent vehicle for organizational stability, in that it helps build trust and credibility, it's also a way to ascertain leadership potential. After all, developing people implies that you're concerned about them and willing to pay attention to what they have to say. In assuming a mentorship role, the leader is not just allowing the mentored person to follow him around, he's also explaining why he's doing what he's doing.

In committing to the process of mentoring, the leader is expanding the reality all those who are being mentored. Eventually, it's up to each individual to take whatever is learned and put their own stamp on it. When that takes place, the uniqueness that everyone can potentially bring to positions of leadership can freely blossom. It's that very blossoming that leads to the energy boost necessary to take poorly performing companies and lift them out of their doldrums.

Niccolo Machiavelli once observed, "The first method for estimating the intelligence of a ruler is to look at the men around him." Developing people is not an act of altruism. *To grow an organization, leaders must grow people. If a leader is able to grow enough people, the degree of influence the leader has within an organization expands exponentially.*

Everyone is ignorant,

only in different subjects.

~ Will Rogers

It's quite natural for a leader to look around and make a judgment about his "bench strength." "Who's on my team, and how good are they?" This is a common question that every perceptive leader asks. When a new leader walks into a dis-eased company, the people he finds on his team may not necessarily be the ones he wants to work with. This situation is often awkward, but it must be handled in short order. The leader needs to act quickly and conscientiously to identify his leadership team and bring it up to speed.

Delaying such decisions almost always proves to be counterproductive. A new leader needs to hit the ground running. First impressions linger for a long time. Getting off to a good start increases the likelihood that things will start moving in the right direction without too much fuss or bother.

People are almost always guarded and apprehensive about a new boss. When counseling top managers, particularly ones who have just come on board, I first urge them to meet regularly, "one-on-one" with every member of their management team, taking lots of notes afterward. It's vital to establish immediate trust and credibility with direct reports. I find that getting this accomplished is not based on knowing all the right answers, but in asking the right questions.

I often suggest that new leaders formulate a list of written questions for their managers to answer. These questions are designed to provide insights into past accomplishments and detail actions taken by the manager that have worked and not worked, as well as ideas about personal "styles" of communication with colleagues and subordinates. This information provides the new boss with an overview of how people on his team see their work universe. By employing this methodology, a lot is revealed in a short period of time.

I have woven a parachute out of

everything broken.

~ William Stafford

Depending on the company culture, other questions might be used—questions involving staff morale, conflict resolution or internal barriers which might prevent the operation from being successful. As always, listening and observation are the keys to gaining greater insight about management bench strength. In addition, assigning specific tasks to certain individuals and paying careful attention as to how those tasks are carried out will yield valuable information and provide insights about whether or not you have "the right people riding on your bus."

Another useful tool for any manager who wants to enhance his leadership role is to explain to subordinates exactly how they go about managing people. There's no reason to keep people guessing about how you manage or what your performance expectations are. Tell them up front about your "hot buttons." Leave nothing to their imagination. Then, if they drift in some way, they'll know what they're drifting from and what your response will be.

This approach doesn't preclude the absence of meaningful dialogue. It helps to know how individuals structure their work and carry out assignments. Good management is a two-way street. Rigidity is not what it's all about—results are the only thing that count. Within this framework, there's plenty of room for input and flexibility. By articulating performance expectations—and sticking to them—the leader is creating a solid foundation for fostering the development of his subordinates. The purpose of standards is to set a performance bar; however, there's no reason why people can't keep moving the bar even higher. The important thing is to first create that bar, then build a momentum which allows direct reports to take that bar to greater heights—on their own volition. When that happens, the leader knows that the energy is flowing the way it should be.

I always wanted to be somebody when I grew up.

I only wish I had been a little more specific.

~ Lily Tomlin

Establishing Congruencies in Job Description, Expectation & Performance

Over the years, I've come to realize that in business it's the simple things that are overlooked. Take for example, job descriptions versus actual job responsibilities. One would think that it's a cut and dry matter—people have job descriptions that spell out what they're supposed to do, and that's that. In reality, nothing could be further from the truth. Job descriptions quite often are poor indications of what an employee is doing or should be doing. It's the job of a leader to make sure that these components are congruent.

Here's a simple two-part test: In the first part, assume your HR Department has job descriptions for every employee. (This might be too much to assume, but let's work with this assumption so we can get to the next part of the test.) Pull three or four of these descriptions from the files at random. Read them over thoroughly. Do these job descriptions say everything that needs to be said about the person's duties and responsibilities? How detailed are the descriptions? Do they talk about specific points of interface with others in the organization? Do the descriptions discuss behaviors that are unique to the job in question?

If there are doubts about any of these questions, hold on to them for a brief moment until the second part of this little exercise is concluded.

Now for Part II: With job description in hand, ask to speak to an employee who works in that position. Sit him or her down and explain that you're conducting a little research experiment, to which there is no right or wrong answer. Then, ask them in as detailed a manner as possible to provide a description of their job—as if they were writing their own job description. At the same time, ask them

A common mistake

when people try to design something

completely foolproof is to underestimate

the ingenuity of complete fools.

~ Douglas Noel Adams

to emphasize what kinds of tasks take up most of their time and who they most often interact with as they carry out their duties.

How accurate is their description relative to the written one? To what extent is their description similar to your idea of what the job performance entails? Now, do a down and dirty assessment: To what extent is the written job description out of alignment with your understanding of the job and the understanding of the employee?

The degree to which these three assessments don't match is the degree to which you, the employee and the organization are barking up different trees. (Let's just hope these trees are in the same field!) The simple truth is that a person cannot lead effectively unless people understand exactly what it is they're supposed to do. If the ship QE II leaves England for New York City and is a few degrees off course, she'll wind up in the Carolinas. The same is true about jobs. If an employee has one notion of what his job responsibilities are, and his boss and the organization have other notions, the idea of what needs to be done becomes muddled and confusing.

If this muddle is spread throughout the operation, chronic dis-eases erupt. These dis-eases take many forms: replication of services and activities, communication problems, overstaffing, understaffing, confused decision making, unfair rewards and recognition, short-sighted planning, no planning, etc., etc. The list of possible ailments is endless.

In addition, there is another issue which arises from such incongruencies. It concerns the ability of the company to properly evaluate performance. Performance evaluations, at their highest level, are mechanisms for growing people. An exceptional performance evaluation provides opportunities to accurately assess a person's strengths and weaknesses. It further enables the manager or supervisor to both coach and monitor performance so that the employee can grow and

Do not fear mistakes - there are none.

~ Miles Davis

become more successful. The sad truth is that, more times that not, performance evaluations are about nothing more than raises or warnings of impending dismissal—all of which are way off target.

The state government agency I worked for early in my job career provides an extreme example of chronic "job description dis-ease." Because the agency was constantly strapped for money, raises were perpetually frozen. Some employees hadn't received a raise in years. According to State Personnel Regulations, the only way a person could earn more money was by changing their job description, usually to reflect some added responsibility, such as supervising another person. In order to reward hard-working people (or favored individuals), a new job description—in actuality, a complete fabrication—was put together.

Eventually, it was discovered that the entire Health Department was grossly out of alignment vis-a-vis what people were paid, what their job descriptions said they were doing and what they were really doing! This huge mess required months to correct, at a staggering cost in both manpower hours and money. In the presence of such chaos, it was impossible to evaluate anyone in good faith. Needless to say, such abuses also engendered a fair degree of bitterness among those who never saw any salary increases. If anyone had a strong intention to manage well, the very system itself became a big hindrance.

Of course, this is an extreme example of job descriptions gone haywire. What usually occurs in for-profit businesses is something more benign, whereby the intentions are good, but the mechanism is faulty. Such was the case with a gaming corporation client of mine that had a reputation for being "people oriented." They had put together a most elaborate performance evaluation protocol—so elaborate, in fact, that it was unworkable. According to the process they developed, an employee was to be evaluated four times a year, or, if you will, once

I shall become a master in this art

only after a good deal of practice.

~ Erich Fromm

every three months. Some supervisors had more than fifty people to evaluate. This made the task impossible to complete right at the outset, despite heroic attempts to complete the task.

To further complicate this woeful situation, the performance evaluation had provisions for correcting deficiencies. But there was never enough time to correct them—nor was there time to address individual concerns or monitor and correct nonproductive behavior. By the time one cycle of evaluations was completed, it was time to begin another! No one had the remotest chance of getting anything done. The entire effort was, for all intents and purposes, a gigantic "make-work" project—one which depleted energy, undermined effective supervision and lowered morale. And because this process was given "sacred cow" status from corporate headquarters, no one ever voiced criticism—although there were hints of dissent whispered in every corridor of every facility.

The concept of growing people as a necessary component for developing leaders is, of course, both important and necessary. However, the right support services and mechanisms must be in place for this to happen. To attempt to grow people by employing actions or programs that are either poorly conceived or ineffectively structured, serves only to infect the operation with more unwanted dis-ease elements.

<u>*Growing People through the Spirit of Play*</u>

Early on in the management and organizational development process, I find it helpful to introduce the subject of play. In one exercise, I ask participants to relate to one another pleasant memories of their childhood play with others. The accent is on pleasant memories (not, for example, the time your brother hit you in the head with a baseball bat).

The creation of something new

is not accomplished by the intellect

but by the play instinct

acting from necessity.

~ C.G. Jung

Participants enjoy this exercise because they can, for a brief moment, recall times when life seemed more open for exploration, fun and experimentation. The stories that come forth are as diverse as the people who tell them—those from urban backgrounds talk about playing in alley ways or in industrial areas, for instance. One fellow used to steal large cardboard boxes from the back door of a kitchen supply company. They would take these boxes, which were used to pack stoves and refrigerators, and convert them into military forts to defend themselves against any and all attackers. Participants from rural areas would talk about evening frog hunts or fishing in alligator-infested waters. The stories are always endlessly fascinating.

The only thing that I can predict with any accuracy about these story tellings is the spontaneous laughter that overtakes participants when they hear about the playful childhood antics of their colleagues. Once the stories are told, I request that participants write down one or two words that best describe the feelings or impressions they experienced during these playful childhood moments.

The words that are most often given include: *fun, adventure, challenge, danger, laughter, courage, craziness, freedom, learning, friendship, winning, exploration, taking chances, acceptance, action, stimulating,* and *trouble-making.* I'm sure you could add many more.

The purpose of all of this nostalgia is to underscore the fact that business-es, especially those which are dis-eased, desperately need a sense of play in their environment. They need to relearn what spontaneity and freedom are about. Effective leadership is largely a matter of creating an environ-ment where work is transformed into play. Take another look at the list of the words italicized above. Many of the people who volunteered these words are CEO's, executives, directors of corporate divisions, managers and supervisors from diverse industries—in short, people who have a vested interest in seeing that their businesses succeed.

It doesn't mean a thing

if it ain't got that swing.

~ Duke Ellington

When we take these words—fun, adventure, courage, challenging, etc.—and begin to apply them to specific actions, behaviors and conditions that effective companies need to possess to be successful, we have created, in essence, a laundry list of "to do's" for anyone who is actively involved in influencing others. For example, what kinds of attitudes need to be in place so that people feel that they are having fun at work, so that it isn't at all drudgery? Or, similarly, what kinds of duties, assignments or interactive involvement can engender a sense of challenge, of learning about new or exciting things?

This is the kind of brain storming that feeds creative leadership and helps to further the process of growing people. By taking a look at each of the words in the "pleasant childhood memory" exercise and determining what their opposites are, other types of brainstorming questions will be elicited. For example, from the antonyms of the words "challenging," "stimulating" and "adventure" we can formulate an insightful question: What aspects of a work environment contribute to feelings of sluggishness, discouragement, boredom, inaction, business-as-usual attitudes, etc.?

A close examination of the implications behind these "opposites" can yield worthwhile insights into what your company needs to fix, modify, change or eliminate entirely. Thinking about these things is a form of creative expression, which is yet another way to grow people and problem solve at the same time.

I have found that the ten Leadership Characteristics introduced in this part are particularly helpful in allowing managers in troubled companies to tackle issues and challenges with more direction and clarity. In emphasizing these characteristics, it's important to realize that teaching people how to lead is more about feeling than thinking. To understand what role—say, compassion or determination—play in influencing others, one must be capable of experiencing these ele-

Any powerful idea is absolutely fascinating -

and absolutely useless unless we

choose to use it.

~ Richard Bach

ments in one's own life. In order to fully grasp the essence of what it means to transpose these vital energies into working environments, one must experience them first hand.

Leadership, in the final analysis, is much more than driving numbers and meeting quotas. It's about exploring people's potential for uniting in pursuit of common goals. It is the triumph of a vision that becomes reality. The Dutch philosopher Erasmus noted that "Fortune favors the audacious." And so it is with leaders, who, unrestrained by convention, are able to boldly move in directions where the fearful will not go. Dis-eased businesses are places that harbor unhealthy amounts of uncertainty and fear. Managing in these settings requires an ability to dance and play with these variables, rather than be paralyzed by them. In doing this, managers transform into authentic leaders.

Now, more than ever before, businesses need revitalization. Through vigorous pursuit of these leadership strategies, businesses of all shapes and sizes will be better prepared to address internal ailments and position themselves for a brighter future.

It takes two to know one.

~ Gregory Bateson

Part Three

Strategy Number Two:
Ending Dysfunction in the Workplace
Through Implementation of
"Strategic Partnering"

*"I don't know what your destiny will be,
but one thing I know: the only ones among
you who will be truly happy are those who
will have sought and found how to serve."*

~ Albert Schweitzer

The year was 1974. I was doing graduate work at the Semmelweis Medical School in Hungary. The psychiatric hospital, where I was assigned, was located on the outskirts of Budapest in a rather remote rural setting. Few cars were seen in this locale, save for an occasional official vehicle and some foreign tourist traffic. Walking one day

All I've learned about life I can

sum up in three words:

It goes on.

~ Robert Frost

through a small village, located about two kilometers from the hospital, I found myself on a long dirt road filled with pedestrians. It was a cloudy, overcast morning. Light rain was falling.

I heard the noise of a car engine. Turning my head, I noticed an official government vehicle making its way down the center of the crowded road. It wasn't moving quickly, so there was ample time for the villagers to get out of the way. I distinctly remember how, when the car passed, everyone fixed their eyes on it, as if they had never seen an automobile before. I found this somewhat strange, but continued walking, even when a group of people had stopped to focus more steadily on the moving vehicle. A few of these observers actually halted their conversations in mid-stream, continuing to gaze at the car as if it were an apparition.

All at once, there was a loud thud. The car had driven into a two-foot trench that stretched across the length of the road. No warning signs of any kind had been posted. It was more than obvious that everyone except the unlucky driver knew the large rectangular rut was there. Why hadn't anyone alerted the driver about the fate that awaited him at the end of that dirt road?

It would have been so easy to send out a warning, yet no one did so. Perhaps it had something to do with the numbness of populations in what was then communist Eastern Europe. I'll never know. Even after the car went nose down into the trench, people remained motionless, fixed within their silent gaze. To this day, as I recall this incident, what stands out in my mind is the complete sense of detachment that the pedestrians exhibited, a detachment that, in view of the impending consequences, was nothing short of unnerving.

People in dis-eased companies detach from one another in much the same way as those Hungarian pedestrians did with that unlucky driver on that rainy afternoon. Clearly, they were interested in what

We make a living by what we get.

We make a life by what we give.

~ Winston Churchill

was going on, but that was the extent of their involvement. People who detach from ongoing actions and events are people who are, by nature, self-protective.

Detachment represents a form of disengagement. It's a way of saying, "I'm not involved," or "I choose not to be associated with this person, (this group, this initiative, etc.)" Detachment can be overt or subtle. In organizational groups, overt detachment is most effectively carried out in turfs. Here, entire groups essentially draw a line in the sand and metaphorically post "DO NOT DISTURB" signs around themselves, their colleagues and their operations.

Overt detachment also occurs when people distance themselves from specific individuals, particularly those who might be targeted for dismissal or are in political disfavor with some or all of the organization's power brokers. By contrast, subtle detachment can occur among both individuals and groups. It's often used as a tactic to give the impression that support and buy-in are present, when in reality little or none exist.

Subtle detachment also takes the form of undermining projects or initiatives. Delaying decisions or being irresponsive to messages, requests or report deadlines are typical examples of subtle detachment. People in organizations usually detach out of a desire to pursue their own agendas—which are almost always self serving in nature.

The most common reasons for individual detachment in business settings are to avoid or deflect responsibility or to distance oneself from an action or situation that is perceived to be damaging or threatening to one's interests. If detachment, as an operative tactic, becomes rooted in a company's culture, it's an indication that the organization has serious issues with trust, credibility and confidentiality—the three "pillars of organizational integrity." And, as has been pointed out, when there is little or no integrity, dis-ease and dis-integration are the inevitable result.

The house of the heart is never full.

~ African Proverb

In western cultures, it's easier to detach from work group processes than in Latin American, Asian or African cultures, where membership in groups helps establish identity and clarify behavioral responsibilities. So much of the rhetoric of North American business is oriented toward the concept of attachment. We call it by another name: teamwork. But authentic teamwork is not so easily accomplished in western business models. Part of the issue has to do with the fact that westerners thrive on individualism. Marketers are keenly aware of this, and are even somewhat responsible for causing it, by targeting specific goods and services to various segments of the population. For example, teenagers have their own TV shows, music, movies, fashion wear, toothpaste, designer cell phones, as do women, men, senior citizens, et. al.

In their book, *The Wisdom of Teams,* Jon Katzenbach and Douglas Smith discuss many conditions that must be present for teamwork to really work. They include: shared responsibility, shared rewards, complementary skills, the ability to spend non-work related time together and a collective determination to succeed. Making teams work requires concentrated efforts and continual reinforcement—something that most organizations don't do very well.

From my own experience, I've seen teams that function fairly well, only to be thwarted by other groups when they reach out for support. Similarly, certain groups that call themselves teams might function decently, but are unable to integrate or reach out to others in a strategic manner. Therefore, much about being successful is contingent upon people being ready and able to function strategically with one another! Frequently, roles and relationships within the team are not well defined. This can often result in dysfunctional relationships, as members jockey for positions of control or clumsily trip over one another's feet while attempting to get things done.

Deep down we must have real affection

for each other, a clear realization of our

shared human status.

~ The Dalai Lama

If teams become a permanent fixture in an organizational structure, there is a tendency for their energy to become stale over time. Teams which are created in order to address short term projects or issues of concern generally have a better shot at succeeding, so long as they meet most of the characteristics of authentic teams that Katzenbach and Smith identified.

It is both sad and true that most business teams exist in name only. After years of observation, I've encountered only a handful of management teams that really functioned as highly skilled, interdependent, well-calibrated groups. Even in those instances, there was always a tendency for these groups to struggle with formulating common goals and objectives. What is truly ironic is that, more often than not, most senior management and executive teams are the most fragmented groups in the operation—which certainly doesn't speak well for how projects are managed or how activities flow within the enterprise.

Teams are frequently thought to be the most desirable vehicles for getting work done. However, having teams in place doesn't necessarily mean that anything really different or innovative is going on. Teams, like individuals, need clear purposes and directions. Unless team members are in complete "sync," they require solid leaders to keep them well oiled. And as we have seen, leadership of this kind is hard to come by. Given these underlying dynamics, we can easily find ourselves back at square one, asking the question: What kind of interaction within our work force will enable our business to keep moving forward?

Divided Kingdoms & Ceremonial Beheadings

At this point, a slight digression is necessary. During the writing of this book, I was invited by an internal human resource executive to visit and talk to the president of a two hundred million dollar a year

Every human being on this earth is
born with a tragedy, and it isn't original sin.
He's born with the tragedy that he has to
grow up. A lot of people don't have
the courage to do it.

~ Helen Hayes

service company about my possible involvement as a consultant to this firm. It seems that the president of this outfit had inherited the job from his father, who founded the company. In recent years, the company had experienced astounding growth and profitability.

The president, as I learned, did not take a terribly active part in the management of his company. What made situations so tenuous was that the company functioned without a COO. When the president did appear in the office, he was usually mobbed by key branch managers, all of whom needed certain decisions to be made.

At our meeting, I was amazed to find that the president was well read in all the current management literature. To hear him talk, you would think that he was the "Moses" of his industry, guiding his flock out of the parched desert into a lush oasis. His comments were riddled with positive metaphors about teams functioning as skilled "oarsmen" all moving rapidly downstream, pointed in the right direction. I must admit, I was impressed. The guy didn't seem to need me at all.

Then I started to ask some pointed questions and make some remarks about accountability. I noticed that as I spoke, the president started to shuffle nervously in his chair, looking at his watch. I instinctively knew what was going on: The last thing in the world that this fellow wanted was to be challenged to "walk his talk." In fact, as I later learned, the last thing that any of his extremely well-compensated branch managers wanted was to work together for a cause greater than the financial success of their own operations, which functioned as if they were feudal kingdoms in relation to one another.

I reasoned that it wouldn't be long before the company's growth would be stymied by its inability to function synergistically nor utilize all of the combined talent to grow the business-at-large.

The hero's will is not that of

his ancestors nor of his society, but his own.

This will to be oneself is heroism.

Life is a desperate struggle to be, in fact,

that which we are in design.

~ Ortega y Gasset

Sometime shortly after this meeting, I received word that my services were not wanted. Out of curiosity, I asked what the difficulty was. The response I received was "bad chemistry." Once again the "God of Bandaids, Quick Fixes and Avoidance" had reared its ugly head. The company in question had so much potential—however, much to the detriment of its hundreds of employees, all it could muster was a group of self-serving managers who could not see beyond the limits of their individual operations. Sooner or later, this myopic stance would take its toll. Successful change is always about harnessing the energy of the collective. For this operation, no such energy was available. Teamwork in this enterprise was nothing more than a series of shallow metaphors, lacking any real meaning or substance.

Apart from disengaged leaders at the top, operations with layered tiers of management also find it difficult to establish a sense of urgency, unity and direction. Those people in middle management, who themselves report to other management tiers, are in particularly awkward situations. Not only are they subject to manipulation by their subordinates, they also find it difficult to get the needed support from their immediate bosses as well as the managers on the next rung of the ladder. Regrettably, these "people in the middle kingdom" often spend their time in "make work projects" designed, in large measure, to justify their own existence.

Who's responsible for this muddle? I'm sure if we try hard we could find a suitable scapegoat, someone to take the rap for all the dis-ease and dysfunction. And it's not surprising to discover that many organizations waste a lot of time doing just that. Sacrificial lambs serve an important function, especially in troubled companies. They enable people to channel large portions of collective guilt and blame on to an individual or group. Once this is done, everybody can take a deep breath, knowing that "those imbeciles have finally been fingered" all

He not busy being born

is busy dying.

~ Bob Dylan

of which serves a worthy purpose, until, of course, the next group of imbeciles take their place.

Sizable numbers of businesses are content to maintain and reinforce these archaic rituals of "purge and renew." Unfortunately, if you've lived through a number of these ceremonial beheadings, it's almost impossible not to become wounded, stale, cynical, frustrated, angry, rebellious or passive. As an organizational/management development "specialist," one of my worst nightmares is to encounter great numbers of these dejected types in the work force.

Working Hard or Hardly Working?

Russell Bishop has noted that in the heating and air conditioning trade, the point on the thermostat in which neither heating nor cooling must operate—around seventy-two degrees—is called "The Comfort Zone." It is also known by another name: "The Dead Zone."

That's the zone wherein these types of wounded employees reside, and that's why perpetually dis-eased businesses are so difficult to cure. When passivity and cynicism runs high, mediocrity rules. Passivity, in particular, produces a unique form of detachment. It is based on a perception of impending negative consequences, in spite of any objective indication that something negative is in the air.

Passive workers (who frequently are in supervisory and managerial positions), do whatever they can to just get by. They usually possess a strong "don't rock the boat" belief system, which, in some businesses, allows them to go unnoticed for long periods of time. (In dysfunctional bureaucracies or highly diseased companies, that period of time can begin on the first day of employment and end on the day of retirement.)

Slow down and enjoy life.

It's not only the scenery you'll miss

by going too fast - you'll also miss the sense

of where you are going and why.

~ Eddie Cantor

The truth of the matter is that large numbers of people in today's labor force, in the presence of poor leadership and ambiguous forms of accountability, are tempted to do as little as possible from one day to the next. The oft heard remark, "Are you working hard, or hardly working?" reflects this underlying sentiment. Individuals who fit this mold, enter a job and find themselves consciously or unconsciously asking the question, "What is the least amount of work I can do, and still not attract the negative attention of my superiors?"

When companies engage in rigorous internal scrutiny they often discover thousands of manpower hours spent in non-work related activities. *This lack of productivity exists in direct proportion to the lack of purpose, mission and accountability within the work culture itself.*

The above scenario is contrasted by its opposite form, namely the worker/manager who is on complete overload, with little or no time for reflection or renewal. In such settings, everything is urgent and nothing can wait. These patterns are particularly common in industries where the corporate office templates all manner of "urgent items" onto an individual's already super-intense work day. Unlike the detached or passive individual, the person on overload has no discretionary time for passivity. People in these settings always feel pressure such that no time exists to prioritize or think strategically. They are victims of a work culture that equates constant activity with forward movement.

I once had the opportunity to travel to the west coast to conduct a workshop, the theme of which focused on "Management During Challenging Times." In the course of this presentation, the area vice president of this Fortune 500 company, the fellow responsible for contracting my services, was forced to leave several times because of corporate demands. These demands so dictated his time that he needed to install a special telephone internet hook-up in our meeting room, so he could continue replying to so-

In a dark time, the eye begins to see.

~ Theodore Roethke

called "urgent" emails, which poured out of headquarters almost by the hour.

I encountered him one evening after a brief dinner break. He announced that he had to retire to his room and continue working for another two hours so as not to fall behind in his work. Similarly, his subordinates, who were all "middle-managers" in the same corporate structure, told me that the demands imposed upon them by the corporate offices were nothing short of overwhelming. The group as a whole appeared to be physically and emotionally exhausted. It was no wonder that they had real trouble thinking about longer range strategic issues.

I've seen these overload patterns among managers and executives grow steadily over the past two decades. Where a quarter century ago the media speculated about how our work force was going to cope with all the leisure time they would be given, the topic of today's conversations is how to maneuver a free weekend to spend quality time with one's family and friends. As a result of technological advances, our lives have become more busy, not less. The idea of personal time has gone almost entirely out the window.

What then, is going on in this maddening work world? Between those who are detached, those who are passive, those who are on overload and those who are manipulating the system for their own purposes, how can one emerge from these systems being both successful and sane? Is there a point of balance which will yield maximum health to our businesses and to ourselves? I believe there is. To accomplish it requires some re-thinking about the nature of relationships within organizations, as well as an understanding of the paramount importance of having a clear sense of purpose and direction. That's what the concept of "Strategic Partnering" is all about.

Golf without bunkers or hazards

would be tame and monotonous.

So would life.

~ B.C. Forbes

The Art of Strategic Partnering

It's no big secret that in the world of management theory and organization development technology, there's really nothing new under the sun. However, with the level of knowledge that now exists in the area of behavioral psychology, group process and motivation theory, there are some fresh ingredients that, if combined properly and given proper emphasis, can offer great potential for balance and success to businesses both large and small. All that's required is a willingness to try to grasp the processes involved, along with a strong sense of determination and persistence in implementing them.

The word "process" is an important one, because it implies a series of actions, functions and changes which, over time, produce the intended results. Any process that is introduced in a business organization will unfold in its own unique way, depending upon a number of variables.

One elemental variable for the success of Strategic Partnering is the presence of leaders who reflect the characteristics that were noted earlier in this book. It seems to be a given that good leadership is a requirement for positive change. It's then not at all unrealistic to propose that part of any effort to effect positive change necessitates the presence of capable leaders.

As has been noted, dis-eased companies are in particular need of solid leadership. They need people who are prepared to address tough issues and make difficult decisions without caving in to naysayers or obstructionists. Therefore, *a necessary part of any attempt to bring about constructive renewal within a dysfunctional operation, regardless of the plan of action, requires a continual effort to recruit and develop people who are comfortable with leadership roles.*

When love and skill work together,

expect a masterpiece.

~ John Ruskin

Primarily, these should be people who understand and are sensitive to behaviors and attitudes that encourage subordinates to abandon old unproductive habits and adapt new approaches for getting things done. The saying, "No one likes change except a wet baby," is at least 85% correct—which means that 15% or more of a company's work force can quickly become the leverage point for change and the shock troops for building a critical mass of followers among those who need extra prodding.

When capable leadership is put into place and an effective plan of action is introduced, it won't be long before results start to appear. Once results take hold, the more employees will begin to experience, first hand, the benefits of change initiatives. From that point onward, the actions which take place are similar to watering, fertilizing and weeding a garden. However, instead of water, fertilizer and weed killer, the company is using group synergy, rewards and strong demands for accountability to grow their results.

The concept of Strategic Partnering, as I conceive it, looks much like a well-choreographed dance. There are a number of movements which must be practiced and rehearsed; there are lead dancers and those who follow; there's even an eye on the audience response—in this case, customers, vendors and any other individuals or entities who interface with the company.

Stretching the metaphor a bit, it could be argued that Strategic Partnering is a "movement piece" which involves intense "audience participation." To understand the basic concepts of Strategic Partnering, I encourage the reader to think carefully about the way certain terms are defined and explained. There's a tendency to take any concept and mold it into a shape that seems to fit the conceptual framework of the person who's absorbing it. For example, take the concept of teamwork that was discussed earlier.

In the confrontation between the stream

and the rock, the stream always wins—

not through strength but

through perseverance.

~ H. Jackson Brown

Teamwork means different things to different people. Therefore, to be able to nail down a definition of teamwork, and not just be satisfied with our own idea about what it means, the word needs to be rigorously qualified.

If I were then to say that, in order to have teamwork, we need team players who a) have worked with one another in the past, b) respect each other's abilities, c) function well together in a work setting, d) share common goals, e) have complimentary skills, f) are content with being rewarded equally and g) have no "control" issues in relation to one another, we would have narrowed our definition by a considerable margin.

Once we obtain a basic understanding of the concepts involved, we needn't burden ourselves with excessive attempts to define everything. Things will begin to flow when common concepts are rigorously defined and reinforced. Given all of the above qualifiers, let's now look at the Strategic Partnering concepts. The nucleus of Strategic Partnering is the formation of PARTNERSHIPS.

The formal dictionary definition of partnership is: "a relationship between individuals or groups that is characterized by mutual cooperation and responsibility, as for the achievement of a specified goal." All well and good. Once again, though, we are tempted to give way to knee jerk responses to words like "mutual cooperation," "responsibility" and "goal." To do that, in this instance, would not take us where we need to go.

Rather, what is desired is a comfortable feel for the underlying meaning of these words. Once this is done, a more realistic frame of reference for the concept of partnership will develop. This, in turn, will allow the organization to form partnerships with high degrees of precision and clarity.

Don't worry about people stealing your ideas.

If your ideas are any good, you'll have to ram

them down peoples' throats.

~ Howard Aiken

Glancing once again at the dictionary, we discover that one definition for "partner" is "either of two persons dancing together." Once we get over our laughter at imagining two guys on a manufacturing floor doing the tango, we discover in this definition the nature of what dancing well with a partner really means. There needs to be coordination, sensitivity, anticipation of movement, a sense of rhythm, flexibility, precise timing and hopefully, a solid dose of energy and enthusiasm. Superb dance partners also understand each other's strengths and weaknesses and can help each another compensate when difficult maneuvers are required. Now we're getting closer to the idea of what a working partnership is all about.

The "Strategic" part of the Strategic Partnership couplet implies that there is a specific plan involved in the enactment of that partnership. One of the essential aspects of that plan is that an "Active Dialogue" be initiated by each partner. This Active Dialogue is on-going. It consists of structured conversations designed to articulate and sometimes hammer out things that each partner needs to understand about what each person is doing, how they're doing it and what kind of support is required.

The term "Active Dialogue" needs to be introduced in the organization as a call for a certain type of conversation. No other term should be used. The purpose is to instill in people the awareness that Active Dialogue, by definition, means there is a need to enhance or clarify the partnership relationship. It's not a call for confrontation; it's not a challenge to a duel; nor is it a request for someone to join you in a mid-day break. Active Dialogues are opportunities to raise important issues, exchange bits of value-added information, clarify tasks, secure buy-in, get feed back and, most importantly, continue to solidify the partnership itself.

The entire business of Active Dialogues will become clearer as we go along. Some formats for Active Dialogues, particularly among groups,

Good judgment comes from experience.

And experience ... well that comes

from poor judgment.

~ Anonymous

should be scheduled or planned in advance. In these instances they are not just meetings, they are "choreographed check-ins." If everything appears to be in place, then the Active Dialogue is complete. Active Dialogues are to the point. Constantly redefining roles or responsibilities implies that the partnership has never really been in full alignment.

It's helpful to look at Active Dialogue as a strategic "huddle." If some things need to be ironed out by two or more members of the Active Dialogue huddle, that's fine. No one else needs to be involved. The reason for all this apparent rigidity is the concurrent need to create a template for action and build an ideological framework for supporting the tasks that the partnerships undertake.

The Anatomy of Strategic Partnerships

Strategic partnerships have two basic component parts. The first is a continuing Active Dialogue centered around issues involving mutual support. The second is the on-going business of mediating the way you want things to look.

In carrying out the first component, one of the partners or groups asks the following question: "How can I support you?" This question is vital, because it allows the other partner(s) to learn about the support that he must provide to permit the other to execute his duties. Partners need to feel confident that they are each getting the support that's needed. Active Dialogue provides the mechanism to build a working "hand and glove" relationship. What takes practice is becoming sensitive to what "supporting someone" really means. Sometimes giving support means providing emotional support—kind words or expressions of validation. At other times, it means brainstorming with your partner about what they're doing and how they're

Would you rather be right or happy ?

~ Jerry Jampolsky

doing it—even to the point of bringing in an outside "specialist" for a more objective analysis.

Every partner needs to understand that he or she is a part of a process, which means that everything is always in flux. There are occasions when one partner or another has an unrealistic view of what support looks like. When that happens, it's up to the partners to make an attempt to work things out. Once again, a neutral party may be needed to provide a balanced perspective. However, a supervisor or manager should only be asked to intervene when the Active Dialogue process falters.

At that point, it's up to that superior to lend a hand and make recommendations about the way support needs to be extended. Like any new type of learning, active dialogues have to be practiced continually. Most staff, especially in dis-eased operations, have little or no understanding of the subtle elements that comprise the act of supporting another. They are usually too busy protecting themselves against real or imagined threats.

Even senior managers have difficulty figuring out the kind of support they need, over and above the larger mandate to "make the numbers and deliver the goods." Consequently, the Active Dialogue which takes place in a Strategic Partnering relationship serves as an on-going vehicle to coordinate, calibrate and fine-tune every type of working relation-ship. Strategic Partnerships are initiated and maintained both vertically and horizontally, throughout the organization. When your boss is your partner, that's a vertical relationship; partnership with a peer is a hori-zontal one. In vertical partnerships, it's imperative that management fully grasps the notion of support with respect to subordinates.

The most difficult part of implementing really effective Strategic Partnerships is the degree of "ego involvement" that is present. By this, I mean the degree to which one or both partners fee

The truth of the matter is

you always know the right thing to do.

The hard part is doing it.

~ Norman Schwartzkopf

they have to be right. Thin-skinned individuals don't make good partners. Partners must learn that they are operating within a "bigger picture" than their own fragile egos. I'll talk more about this shortly.

If we look back to the Fleet Management case study presented in the first part of the book, it was the vertical partnership between supervisor and mechanic that made the team concept workable. No longer was the supervisor an arbitrary, malevolent dictator. In his transformed role, he became an active part of the team, in that he served as a vital resource person for the team's needs, as well as the person who helped mediate work load assignments. In turn, the support that the supervisor needed required that each individual have a clear idea of how to provide a fair day's work, along with the assurance that the work performed would meet the high quality standards that the department set in place.

I recall one high-tech business where I introduced the Strategic Partnering concept. The employees were, almost to the person, independent self-starters. They knew what they had to do. And it was easy for them to determine how their peers needed to be supported. The problem that existed for them was this: their supervisors didn't really know what support for these subordinates looked like. In this particular situation, it was the absence of a strategic link between worker and front line supervisor that was causing problems.

Specifically, the technicians in this outfit wanted to receive more timely information about changes in policy or procedures. Further, they wanted the supervisor to go to bat for them in getting Human Resources to respond to questions involving things such as benefits, sick leave, time off, errors in paychecks, etc.—things which the supervisor could accomplish with relative ease, if he had an intention to do so, which many did not.

An investment in knowledge always

pays the best interest.

~ Benjamin Franklin

In one gaming resort I worked with, the staff members wanted supervisors to give them more feedback on how they were doing, prior to any written assessment. Further, they requested assistance in helping people transfer to other areas, if they had the needed skills. Lastly, realizing that the more you knew the more you were worth, they requested more cross-training opportunities, whenever possible. All of these were fair requests—and some supervisors attended to these issues because they felt it was their duty. Most, unfortunately, ignored them, and the result was constant bickering and fragmentation.

Arguably, these issues could have been addressed without utilizing a Strategic Partnering umbrella. However, having that umbrella as an operative framework enabled these requests to take place without having to beg or complain. Without the Strategic Partnering initiative, a casino employee was lucky if a supervisor attended to such "trivial details" at all. Through the Active Dialogue process and the accountability for action that accompanied it, a system was put into place that improved the entire way in which supervisors related to line staff, and vice-versa.

It's often said that "the Devil's in the details." I would add that these details are contained in every subtle interaction that might define what it looks like for one person to support another. Dysfunction often results when these supportive elements are ignored or undervalued. En totto, they constitute the fine points of what on-purpose performance is all about. Without them, things chug along in their usual mediocre fashion, without much variation. The use of Active Dialogue serves as an indispensible tool for increasing the probability that exceptional actions will become the norm.

An attorney friend of mine, who is a stickler for detail, frequently quotes an old adage: "For the want of a nail, the shoe was lost—the shoe that was affixed to the front hoof of the Commanding General's horse. In battle, the horse stumbled. The General fell and was killed.

The easiest kind of relationship for me

is with ten thousand people.

The hardest is with one.

~ Joan Baez

The battle was lost, and the course of history changed." Obsessive compulsive types love this adage. I, myself, like it because it demonstrates how seemingly minor oversights can result in a dramatic change in outcomes. Everything, you see, is ultimately linked to everything else. This is no less true in places of business than in life in general. Strategic Partnerships are the nails that hold the shoe firmly on the Commanding General's horse. The implications here are more than obvious.

Deciding whether partnerships should be created between two people or among groups is not so much the issue as making sure that the active dialogues in place are truly supportive in nature. I recommend that everyone in an organization have at least two or three "one-on-one" partners, depending upon the nature of the job. *Active dialoguing in the manner prescribed is capable of producing strong personal bonds, and equally strong linkages between tasks and responsible action.*

Two-person "dyads" can produce highly coordinated and even intuitive professional relationships. That's why it's good to have many dyadic relationships at upper management levels. Given the nature of management hierarchies, upper level managers have much broader spans of control than their lower echelon colleagues, which means that their ability to influence large numbers of people is also operative. In requiring upper level managers to follow "horizontal" Strategic Partnerships, critical synergistic relationships are encouraged.

These synergistic relationships, especially at higher management levels, are purposely meant to help dissolve the grandiose egos that frequently dominate the executive corridors of enterprises, both large and small. I'm sure all of us are aware that turf wars and in-fighting are themselves direct by-products of egos gone wild. It's also

In the end, we will remember

not the words of our enemies,

but the silence of our friends.

~ Martin Luther King, Jr.

commonly acknowledged that the clash of egos has destabilized a number of corporate entities in the recent past—General Motors, AOL/Time Warner and Coca Cola are just a few among many which come to mind.

It's important to bear in mind that Strategic Partnerships should not be aggregated to more than about eight to twelve people, at most. Otherwise, the chances are too great that on-purpose communication, tactical thinking and supportive responsibilities will dissipate. This doesn't mean that everyone in an organization shouldn't act in the spirit of partnership with everyone else. However, Strategic Partnerships, by their very nature, entail very detailed and task-oriented forms of Active Dialogue—meaning that smaller is better.

The businesses where I've instituted Strategic Partnering initiatives, seemed, over time, to have developed a high degree of "camaraderie" through the workings of the partnerships themselves. The main feature of this camaraderie has been a solid level of trust and an openness in dealing with challenging issues. You might say that a "Strategic Partnering Culture" feels friendlier, more relaxed and open. And that is the elemental foundation for handling most challenges that a business might encounter.

There is no doubt in my mind that implementing Strategic Partnering concepts in dis-eased businesses impacts the company in significantly positive ways. One great benefit is that when the concept takes hold within a company's culture, it's easier to detect people who don't fit well into the operation. In practice, Strategic Partnering seeks to get the very best from a diversity of input. This is accomplished directly by the partnerships themselves, which serve to harmonize and balance energies that are inherent in diverse groups of people.

Concern should drive us into action

and not into depression.

~ Karen Horney

The Importance of a Clear Vision

Now that I've outlined the nature of Active Dialogue and explained the on-going process of understanding each person's idea of how support needs to be given, we enter upon the most crucial part of the Strategic Partnering process—creating a vision. I've dealt with the subject of vision a number of times, but only hinted at its significance in moving an organization out of dis-eased states. It's time now to look at the concept of vision as a more concrete phenomenon.

When I first heard the word "vision" used in an organizational setting, it appeared to me to be a lofty kind of word. Saints and holy people have "visions," as do those who are hallucinating or delusional. This much I could account for. But what about a "company vision?" Perhaps this was something that emanated from a saintly corporate president or a delusional CEO? Whatever its source, the concept of vision seemed to be related to some ideal or even idealistic form—imaginable, but always out of reach.

Strategic Partnerships invoke visions as well. However, they are anything but lofty. For our "strategic" purposes, let's not look at vision in a singular or grandiose sense. Let's regard our vision as something that contains many smaller visions. Each smaller vision represents those elements that a group decides it wants its working environment to look like. Some components of this vision might include: how people need to be accountable, how conflicts or disagreements are handled, what customer service (both internal and external) should look like, what's involved in making sound decisions, what quality in the operation looks like, meeting formats and other significant aspects of one's work environment.

In Strategic Partnering, the vision of "how things should look" is, once again, approached through Active Dialogue. It remains to be

Always listen to the experts.

They'll tell you what can't be done and why.

Then do it.

~ Robert Heinlein

seen whether these dialogues are carried out by the immediate supervisor, another manager, the work group or external facilitators. These decisions depend upon a number of different variables, not the least of which is the leadership acumen of the managers, the company culture and the type of work performed. Regardless of who guides or initiates the vision content, the purpose is to secure complete understanding and buy-in.

The visions, once articulated, become the foundation for evaluating performance, managing people properly and fine-tuning the operation itself. It might be argued that the dialogue process takes too much time. My experience has demonstrated that if dialogues become built into a daily structure and are not set apart as distinct and separate formats, after a short time, they unfold smoothly. Sometimes a bit of external facilitation is required to jump start the process. However, once the active dialogues begin to gain momentum, they pave the way for the complex process of spelling out how things need to operate for the group as a whole. Both the support dialogues and the visioning dialogues serve to continually reshape and modify the work environment in lieu of changing conditions and mandates for action.

The Active Dialogue process may sometimes be introduced by formulating a series of questions to staff to advance or shape a work initiative. These questions need to address potential methods for giving and receiving support, as well as provide, in clear terms, what kind of group energy is required for success. Often, these questions can be gleaned through internal focus groups. Under the right circumstances, they can be generated by the group itself.

Once a clear vision is in place and people have given their buy-in, there's not much left to the imagination except to continually review what is agreed upon. It's then the manager's job to make sure that what is agreed to is enacted.

Your motive in working should be

to set others, by your example,

on the path of duty.

~ Bhagavad-Gita

When people buy-in to a vision, they also buy in to the consequences that result from diverting from what was agreed to. The work group has much leeway in deciding how individual deviation is handled. Bear in mind that the "glue" that holds all this together is based upon sound, consistent leadership, combined with the strength and clarity of the vision and the adherence of the employees to that vision.

In Strategic Partnering groups I've facilitated, there have existed a positive connection between members, one that fosters a willingness to support collective efforts. Over time, positive identification with collective goals and objectives exerts strong peer pressure on individuals who might want to create their own distinct set of operating norms. Peer pressure is a powerful force, more so than arbitrary attempts to bring people into line, which is a common occurrence in operations where there is a lot of dysfunction.

Apart from other factors, the entire Active Dialogue process is designed to provide work groups with a sense of control, input and empowerment. The concept of active dialogues, both in pairs and small groups, doesn't merely encourage individual participation, it demands it. However, the idea of empowering employees gives some people the idea that all decisions are controlled at the line level.

That's simply not true. Managers and supervisors up and down the organizational ladder are required to participate fully in the role of leaders—guiding discussions, influencing decision making, monitoring group performance, coaching, clarifying tasks and providing support for all concerned. What exists, in actuality, is a program that balances and harmonizes relationships throughout the workplace, that provides opportunities for flexibility and input from employees and supportive leadership from supervisors and managers, all at the same time.

A crank is a man with a new idea—

until it catches on.

~ Mark Twain

Balance is one of the critical elements which is so desperately needed in dysfunctional companies—especially those where workers feel extreme disempowerment amidst fragmented management.

The methodology of Strategic Partnering provides an understandable framework for combating this type of disintegration. The manner in which Strategic Partnering concepts are introduced plays a large role in determining how quickly and successfully the program will take hold.

Let's look at two contrasting work groups to gain a clearer picture of how this process might be introduced. Imagine, if you will, a small group of men and women working in some kind of for-profit business. They are all relatively bright, and, for the most part, dedicated to doing a good job. Each of them believes they are doing the best job they can. However, after close scrutiny, it's discovered that a few of them need to work a little harder, a few others don't communicate well with co-workers and several others seem to have broad interpretations about how policies and procedures should be implemented. Within this setting, everyone appears cordial—no one is really rocking the boat, so together they form a status quo profile.

This environment provides decent job benefits. People willingly contribute to company sponsored charities, social causes and the like. There are several annual company events, including a big Christmas party and a summer picnic, where everyone's family is invited. These events are always well attended. The particular work group in question has a middle-aged female as a boss. She has been with the company a number of years and has risen up from the ranks.

Her peers and subordinates describe her as pleasant, easy going and fun to work with. She's not really into details, so everyone works more or less independently. People like this approach, because they

I am never weary of being useful ...

in serving others I cannot do enough.

No labor is sufficient to tire me.

~ Leonardo da Vinci

are left alone. On the whole, their collective performance is acceptable, but far from stellar.

Now, imagine a second work group. They are composed of primarily self-serving individuals, each of whom has their own agenda, some of which are known, others of which are pursued covertly. Only a few have any respect for their manager, who has the reputation for being a micro-managing, authoritarian "S.O.B." He is inclined toward favoritism, and is prone to angry outbursts. Basically, his subordinates try to avoid him as best they can. If forced to interact, they find themselves agreeing with everything he says, in knee-jerk fashion. However, as soon as his back is turned, they do what they want, all the while giving the appearance of acquiescence.

Some of the weaker employees in this group are fearful for their jobs, never knowing when the ax might fall. They are plagued by anxiety and dislike their jobs intensely, but are unsure of their options. The company culture is characterized by pessimism and uncertainty. People generally distrust their bosses. The company offers sub-par benefits. Rewards and raises are few and far between. Overall, their collective performance is borderline acceptable. However, given the extreme mediocrity of the entire company, it's unlikely that any effort will be made to encourage improved performance.

Neither of these two work groups are likely to win any awards. The first group coasts along, while the second struggles with numerous issues. Both groups are getting by—which means they are not doing so badly that they would arouse the attention of higher ups.

Here are two examples of work settings which are familiar to most of us. Neither is extremely dysfunctional, as was the case with studies that were cited previously. Yet both, in their own ways, are falling way short of what they could be doing if they were strategically aligned.

Do not wait for the last judgment,

it takes place every day.

~ Albert Camus

As such, both groups would benefit greatly from a Strategic Partnering initiative. In each profile, the one basic element that both groups share is ineffective leadership. True, the work environments of each group are quite different. Yet the emphasis in both instances must be directed on reframing the leadership initiative.

Introducing Strategic Partnering first to managers allows the concepts of partnership to be initially analyzed and evaluated by the people who are themselves responsible for decision making. In the two scenarios that I just described, both managers face challenges in terms of their ability to grasp the essence of what a Strategic Partnership looks like. The primary challenge of the manager in the first profile is to grasp the fact that maintaining harmonious relationships with subordinates is only one component of successful management. Other important components, such as an ability to define high performance standards, insure accountability and to assist in creating a dynamic vision of success, must be realized if the work team has any chance of climbing past its mediocrity.

The manager in the second work environment profile needs to establish trust and credibility among his subordinates before effective partnering and visioning can begin. In fact, given the wounding that he has already inflicted, a turn-around might not even be possible. The reason his task is so difficult is that through his actions, he has essentially alienated his subordinates. Their non-trusting attitudes have given way to knee-jerk responses that are solely defensive and protective in nature.

In this case, fear-based leadership has created an environment where the only strategy is the strategy to survive. It's somewhat doubtful that such a manager is capable of "changing his stripes." Nevertheless, I have seen instances where managers of this ilk have risen to the occasion and were able to form qualitatively different relationships with subordinates. However, just like animals who have been abused, it's

For this is the journey that men make:

to find themselves. If they fail in this,

it doesn't matter much

what else they find.

~ James A. Michener

difficult for people who have been subjected to overly harsh and some-times arbitrary management styles and decision making, to want to form more open (and therefore more vulnerable) relationships with managers who have not themselves been open and available. As such, it is often more practical in these instances to introduce the Strategic Partnering concepts to mixed groups of managers and line staff, so that authoritative types of managers can have the opportunity to begin a transformational process directly with their subordinates.

The principles of Active Dialogue, visioning and mutual support, which comprise the foundation blocks for effective Strategic Partnering, act as "wake up calls" for many managers and line employees alike, because the principles themselves provide a mirror for people to look carefully at their behaviors and, in so doing, develop a clearer under-standing of how off the mark they have been.

Working with a group of engineers for a firm that produces microchips, I was surprised at those individuals who most effectively grasped the Strategic Partnering concepts—relishing the idea of partnership and the principles of Active Dialogue. Some of them initially appeared to me to be rather "shut-down." However, when given a viable frame-work for communication and a contextual set of guidelines for giving and receiving support, they blossomed.

Referring back to the group profiles that were outlined above, even though one might be persuaded that the "easy going" manager in the first group would adapt well to Strategic Partnering—more so than her authoritarian colleague in group two—experience has shown that outcomes are unpredictable.

Many managers who are dictatorial and authoritarian assume this posture because of deep insecurities about their abilities, coupled with a relative paucity of decent training in how to manage people.

You out there ... so secret.

What makes you think you're alone ?

~ Thomas McGrath

When given a skills-based approach that targets specific desired attitudes and behaviors, placing it the context of a "vision of how we want things to look," they are sometimes able to relax and enjoy the partnering process.

In a relatively short period, the act of dialoguing in partnership enables both employees and managers to reduce the amount of artificial posturing that typically characterizes business relationships. People are able to more comfortably take off their masks and begin to communicate in purposeful ways.

Conflict and Communication

What makes Strategic Partnering so fundamentally distinct from other organizational change concepts is its relentless focus on changing unproductive patterns of communication. Anyone who has raised or is raising teenage children knows what dysfunctional communication is all about. The parent says something. The teenager either responds with a superficial nod of the head or issues forth a blank stare into space. The parent, unsure that the message has been received, either becomes angered or asks once again, "Did you hear what I just said?" If he's lucky, the teenager will mumble a muted "yes." The end result? You've gotten no where fast. Ironic as it may seem, the kinds of "communication disconnects" which characterize parent-teenager exchanges abound in the workplace.

Sometimes the role of the teenager is assumed by the manager or supervisor; sometimes they reverse roles. At other times, they both act out the teenager role. It should be added that this level of communication is not confined to individuals in unskilled jobs. I've personally witnessed these kinds of exchanges among scientists, academicians and high positioned executives. Scary, but true!

Never apologize for showing feeling.
Remember that when you do so you
apologize for truth.

~ Benjamin Disraeli

One of the outstanding by-products of the Active Dialogue process is its usefulness in mediating disagreements or conflicts. Companies that are dis-eased have many troubling symptoms. One of the worst, and most destructive for the organization, is that very few people willingly acknowledge they are wrong or that they've made a mistake. Defensive posturing wastes enormous time and energy and disrupts focus and intention. Untold numbers of managers and line staff will spend countless work hours trying to prove that they are right and someone else is wrong. I'm not merely referring to incidents that mushroom out of control and land on the desk of the Director of Human Resources, I'm referring to incidents that are either misinterpreted, misunderstood or misguided, that occur on a moment-to-moment basis, causing people to emotionally disconnect with one another.

Such common events rarely ever reach the door of the Personnel or Employee Relations Manager. Take for example, an event which occurred years ago when I was on assignment with the then Digital Equipment Corporation, or "DEC," as it was known. Two managers who both had important hand-glove relationships could not see eye to eye on anything. Neither expressed any dislike for the other, but it was apparent that they could not cooperate well with one another. This situation was affecting both their intact organizations, in subtle and overt ways. After much discreet probing, it finally came out that one of the parties in question felt the other had made a disparaging remark about the other's religious orientation. That, in itself, was enough to shut down productive communication for both operational divisions!

Because the DEC culture was supposedly one that was open to expressing ideas and disagreements, no one would have suspected that one seemingly off-the-cuff remark could provoke such an operational disconnect. Given the culture of the company, it was right and proper to assume that the problem was, in some shape or form, a systemic one. Eventually, after much cajoling, I learned what the real

Only threats are frightening;

one soon comes to terms with facts.

~ Oswald Spengler

source of this disconnect was. It took quite a bit of informal persuasion for the offended individual to consider airing her grievance with her colleague. I suggested that she employ the following technique that I've now incorporated into the Active Dialogue process, a technique for resolving issues. The technique is as follows:

1. Approach the party in question by sincerely saying, "I need your help."

2. Explain the situation or incident in as objective a way as possible. Don't make any accusatory statements.

3. Without acting out your feelings, express what you felt or how you are now feeling.

4. Talk about the consequences to you or your operation as a result of the circumstance. Be objective and realistic.

5. Ask the person, "Please let me know what you think about this."

6. KEEP QUIET, and LISTEN CAREFULLY TO WHAT THE PERSON HAS TO SAY.

7. If the situation leads to a dialogue, which in turn, leads to a reasonable resolution, fine. That should be the end of it. If not, say to the person, "I need to think more about your response." Don't argue further.

8. If it is a work related matter, the course of action might involve seeking an "arbiter" or management superior for an "objective" resolution.

There are people who

take the heart out of you,

and there are people who put it back.

~ Elizabeth David

Like all conflict resolution techniques, this one is not perfect. However, when people become used to the Active Dialogue process, with its give and take exchanges and skill-based listening techniques, more objectivity is possible. Beginning the dialogue by sincerely asking for the person's help is a gambit which provokes emotional receptivity rather than defensiveness. By explaining the situation without emotion, in as objective a way as possible, the other party has a chance to view the incident without the usual knee-jerk retaliatory response. Expressing the feelings that you had or have, without acting them out, removes the "hot charge of emotion" from those feelings. Yet because they are given expression, the feeling state itself is validated in the mind of the other. Talking about the consequences of the action or circumstance allows the other party to step into your shoes for a moment and develop a better appreciation of how that incident affected you or your work.

Then, by allowing the other person time to reply, without demonstrating any resistance, you give the person the opportunity to respond to all that has been said. This reflective pause works wonders. Let me reiterate: this is not a fool proof system. But, when linked to the other partnering processes, it serves as a healthy mechanism for detailing the perceived facts while keeping the emotions and negative perceptions in check. If the issue is not resolved, there is at least a good possibility that the potential volatility contained within it will be significantly reduced.

This technique of defusing potential conflict was once introduced to a group of hotel executives and managers who were in the process of opening a new upscale hotel. At the time, the property's chief engineer was at constant loggerheads with one of the hotel's contractors. In fact, they had almost come to blows on one occasion. Several days after I talked about this technique, the chief engi-

It is necessary to any originality

to have the courage to be an amateur.

~ Wallace Stevens

neer approached me. He was a physically big guy, who had a thick east coast accent. He came from a family of laborers and had a gruff, no-nonsense demeanor.

"Doc," he said, "I gotta talk to you. You know that business about solving problems you talked about? Well, I used it with that contractor guy I told you I've been fightin' with." The engineer went on to describe the incident: It seems that after a new carpet was laid in the hotel foyer, the contractor's men came in to finish some plastering. They didn't take time to properly wipe their shoes, and on the way out, they trekked dirt and plaster debris on the new carpet. Discovering what had happened, the chief engineer saw red. He stormed his way over to the contractor's trailer. On the way there, he thought about the problem solving dialogue. Much to his credit, he decided to put the technique to the acid test. Opening the door, and doing everything in his power to hold back his explosive temper, he walked up to the contractor, bit his tongue, took a deep breath and said in a relatively low key voice, "Frank, I need your help."

After that, he dutifully followed all of the instructions I had provided. Then he carefully described the situation, and said, "Frank, what do you think?" He held his breath and remained silent. "Joe," came the reply, "I think we screwed up big time. I'll send my guys over there to clean it up; if we can't get it back to where it was, I'll take whatever it costs out of my pocket."

The chief engineer almost passed out on the spot. "It's a garden variety miracle," he blurted out. Actually, it wasn't a miracle. It was Active Dialogue at work. Everyday businesses carry out millions of professional communication exchanges each day. While they vary in scope and relative importance, all are designed to keep the organization on the move, with an energy and intent that yields positive

Take what you can use

and let the rest go by.

~ Ken Kesey

results. We know from our own day-to-day work experiences that a good percentage of these professional exchanges are faulty, with some being disastrous.

The way a company communicates internally and with its customers and outside vendors plays a huge role in determining success or failure. All of us are familiar with the fact that petty exchanges that go awry can create a downward spiraling energy that can lead to serious dysfunctions. Concentrating on the details and formats of communication is a necessary tool for reversing the gross misunderstandings that characterize a business in decline. Active Dialogue seeks to shape communication so misunderstanding and false perceptions are minimized, allowing more energy and focus to be placed on planning and creative expression.

I'm often impressed by the instinctual "wisdom" of animals. They seem to do things which aid themselves and each other without having to ponder over every detail before acting. Good habits—that is, behaviors which are repeated and produce beneficial outcomes for both the individual and the group—are fundamental goals of the Strategic Partnering process. The intention is always to reinforce such behaviors so they become almost instinctual, like the wise behavior of many animals.

Not long ago, I received a circulated letter about the behavior of geese. Along with detailing certain actions, the piece explained specific bits of wisdom that we can learn from these wonderful feathered creatures. After rereading the piece, I decided that many of these behaviors were ones that applied to the goals of Strategic Partnering. I've taken the liberty to add my own comments to these descriptions. I believe they provide us with another helpful way to view the partnering process. Here it is:

One can never consent to creep

when one feels an impulse to soar.

~ Helen Keller

STRATEGIC LESSONS FROM GEESE

BEHAVIOR #1:

*As each goose flaps its wings, it creates an uplift
for the birds that follow. By flying in a 'V' formation,
the whole flock adds 71% greater flying range than
if each flew alone.*

COMMENTARY:

These geese apparently know far more about the strategic effects
of synergy than their human counterparts. The dictionary tells us
that "synergy" is "the interaction of two or more agents or forces, so
that their combined effect is greater than the sum of their individual
effects." That's what happens when individuals and groups interact
to form working partnerships. They are no longer groups or teams in
name only. The geese may not be aware of the fact that they are adding a full seventy-one percent to their flying range, but I'm sure they
know that the going is much smoother, with less wear and tear upon
any one bird. When Strategic Partnering takes hold, there is more
ease of motion. Carrying out tasks seems less burdensome and ener-
vating. The "V" formation which the geese employ can be likened to
the pursuit of a common set of visions, which assist the collective to
move forward easily and rapidly.

The actions which a collective undertakes is similar to the geese
flapping their wings. Every action that unfolds with a focus on the
collective vision adds the needed "uplift" to achieve targeted results.
The "V" formation also indicates a sense of collective unity, where
each bird understands the intrinsic force of the whole. Likewise,

You know what happens to scar tissue.

It's the strongest part of your skin.

~ Michael R. Mantell

when a feeling of unity manifests in a business enterprise, there is a corresponding sense of serving and being served. That energy alone produces enormous clarity, drive and purpose.

BEHAVIOR #2:

When a goose falls out of formation, it suddenly feels the drag of flying alone. It quickly moves back into formation to take advantage of the lifting power of the bird immediately in front.

COMMENTARY:

It's no fun to feel alienated and isolated in a work setting. Such conditions can lead to low moods and a corresponding lack of focus. Dis-eased companies have scores of employees who feel just like that. Their thoughts and actions are almost entirely defensive in nature. After a while, even if they manage to hold on to their jobs, a feeling of numbness sets in. It's impossible to think or act with purpose or integrity when you've shut down. Like a goose flying alone, the employee in isolation feels disempowered; there's no supportive energy to help him channel his activities. In short, it's a "drag" flying alone. Effective partnerships create meaning, purpose and direction. If the individual strays or falters from collective group efforts, there are mechanisms to bring him back into formation. Coaching and active dialogues are two of the most powerful tools that can and should be used.

The partnerships in the Strategic Partnering Initiative are proactive. Their influence is based on the power of positive communication, combined with dynamic expressions of energy directed toward com-

There's no point in burying the hatchet

if you're going to put up

a marker on the site.

~ Sydney Harris

mon sets of visions. Within these types of work settings, there is an awareness that the group exists to support and not condemn individual performances. Every person has the right to opt out of "formation." However, they need to know that if this is their choice, they will probably have to exit from the group.

There are people whose personalities demand that they "go it alone." There's nothing wrong with that. However, complex organizations need to have the kind of coordinated efforts that can only be realized when the collective acts in sync. Individual ideas are always welcomed, and actively encouraged, but the individual needs to understand that he is always part of a group effort. Individualism, particularly in the presence of self-centered agendas, can be fragmenting and divisive. That's why consensus and commitment are so important to the success of any Strategic Partnering initiative.

BEHAVIOR #3:

When a goose gets sick or wounded, two geese drop out of formation and follow it down to help and protect it. They stay with it until it is able to fly agaim. Then they launch out on their own with another formation, or catch up with their own flock.

COMMENTARY:

Standing shoulder-to-shoulder when the going gets tough, and offering assistance when someone is faltering, is the hallmark of a strong operation. To know that help is available when needed is deeply reassuring. It's that kind of commitment that allows strategic partners to take calculated risks.

Growth is the only evidence of life.

~ Cardinal Newman

In the company of strong, dedicated partners, individually based fears are less prevalent than they would be if a person was alone and struggling to maintain equilibrium. Partnerships significantly reduce the fear factor that prevents individuals from thinking with imagination and foresight. Strategic Partnerships encourage expressive thought. Trial and error is an effective way for an organization to not only remain competitive, but to make big advances.

If the individual fails, it's not the end of the world—or the end of a career. The collective energy which is capable of embracing failure is part of the same energy which relishes and celebrates success. Through the generation of new ideas, and belief in the legitimacy of creative visioning, Strategic Partners help each individual to become the very best they can be.

BEHAVIOR #4:

When a leader gets tired, it rotates back into formation, and another goose flies at the point position.

COMMENTARY:

In Strategic Partnering, leadership is never confined to the highest tiers of management. Leaders are groomed at all levels within the organization. No one person is responsible for success. It takes many people, assuming many types of leadership roles, to accelerate a tired, troubled business enterprise. The energy of one or two leaders cannot elevate a dis-eased business from its operational morass. Leadership needs to be exercised everywhere, from the rank and file to the offices of the president and CEO.

Everywhere people ask,

"What can I actually do?"

The answer is as simple as it is disconcerting;

We can, each of us, work to put our own

inner house in order.

~ E.F. Schumacher

Strategic Partnering nurtures positive interdependence. It values the skills, talents and unique gifts of every organizational player. It recognizes that leadership potential is abundant. As such, there is a calculated intention to expand leadership roles, so that many individuals can demonstrate their capacity to lead. Helping the organization move through obstacles by influencing others to put forth their best efforts needs to be placed at the top of the list of important things that leaders must focus upon.

Leaders, working in a Strategic Partnering initiative, influence people by helping them to dream about what success looks like. It's up to the collective to help make those dreams become reality. As Walt Disney said, "If you can dream it, you can do it."

BEHAVIOR #5:

The geese flying in formation "honk" to encourage those up front to keep up their speed.

COMMENTARY:

As an adolescent, I remember reading books like *Frankenstein* and *Treasure Island*. At this young age, I never fully realized the full implication of the things I read. For example, in Mary Shelly's *Frankenstein*, the monster says, "I am malicious because I am miserable; if any being felt emotions of benevolence toward me, I should return them a hundred fold." What an articulate statement for a monster! Troubled businesses are filled with Frankenstein monsters, who, in the absence of simple acts of recognition and support, become highly disenchanted, and sometimes disruptive, employees.

The present is great with the future.

~ Gottfried Leibnitz

Having attentive, concerned partners greatly reduces the tendency of individuals to become negative toward one's colleagues. The geese that honk in formation are doing more than just encouraging the others to keep up speed. They're also saying, "Hey, I'm here behind you .... you're doing a great job up front, and we support you!" That's the kind of "honking" Strategic Partnering encourages.

The philosopher William James noted, "The deepest principle of human nature is the craving to be appreciated." That principle should not be lost when people enter the work force. If appreciation is lacking, a feeling emerges, either conscious or unconscious. The feeling is that one's life is wasting away—that opportunity and personal growth have all but vanished. Some people manage to hide these sentiments, but they are there nonetheless.

When enough people begin to reflect these disparaging feelings, the ability of a company to maintain positive momentum steadily declines. The evidence that these forces have gained control appears not just in expressions of low morale, but in sinking profitability, apart from any external market conditions.

In years spent attempting to untangle dis-ease in "sick" companies, I can say with candor that I am able to actually feel the negative energy in a dis-eased business. At times, it takes only minutes to pick up a raft of unhealthy "vibes." Unlike our flying geese, there is no energetic honking going on in these work sites.

By contrast, having committed partners and sharing common goals produces an abundance of "happy honkers." Aside from significant variables like innovative thinking, strong leadership and loyal, dedicated employees, developing and maintaining supportive energy gives an organization an enormous competitive advantage. Strategic Partnering acknowledges this potential and seeks to capitalize on its strength.

Experience, which destroys innocence,

also leads one back to it.

~ James Baldwin

In a similar vein, Strategic Partnering is about mobilizing a work force in pursuit of common interests. When groups of people come together and map out strategies to pursue common interests, a functional community is born. At this juncture, only imagination and intention determine the degree of success and abundance that the enterprise is capable of achieving.

Life must be lived as play.

~ Plato

Part Four

Strategy Number Three:
Developing and Harnessing Insight
A New Look At "The Glass Bead Game"

*"As more people achieve some degree of mental calm,
insight or the ability to transform negative emotions
into positive ones, there will be a natural reinforcement
of basic human values and consequently a greater chance
for peace and happiness for all."*

~ The Dalai Lama

In the midst of the Second World War, 1943 to be exact, the great Swiss German novelist Hermann Hesse (1877-1962) penned his seminal work. It was originally titled *Das Glasperlenspiel,* or, *The Glass Bead Game.* To English speaking readers the book became known as *Magister Ludi—The Master Player.* The story takes place

One doesn't discover new lands without

consenting to lose sight of the shore.

~ Andre Gide

in an imaginary province called "Castilia," which is part of a larger country.

Castilia is a very special place. It's where the Glass Bead Game is played. The entire country places much of its focus on fostering an environment that encourages mastery of the game. Only the brightest and most competent people in the kingdom are sent to Castilia to learn how it is played. The story, as it unfolds, follows the life of Joseph Knecht, from his early childhood through his life as a scholar and humanitarian. It culminates with Knecht being named "Magister Ludi," the Master Player of the Glass Bead Game.

Hesse, himself, never tells us how the game works. All we know is that in the act of playing, wisdom and integrity are generated. Hesse implies that because the culture of the country actively supports the Glass Bead Game, prosperity abounds. The values that the game engenders provide for internal peace, social harmony and creative expression for all who reside in the kingdom.

Castalia is a country that has a true appreciation for diversity. It's a place that searches for ultimate wisdom. The ideals of the Glass Bead Game seductively appeal to all those who seek harmony and balance in the world. As we begin to evaluate our business climates, and view the levels of dysfunction and self-centered agendas that clutter its landscape, the values put forth by Hesse seem appealing, but somewhat idealistic. Or are they?

And, if indeed, they are idealistic, should we not still embrace them as an example of what we need to strive for? Exactly what kind of shift would be necessary to move from a position of merely reducing organization dysfunction to one of supporting a sense of social consciousness, in which everyone shares the benefits?

Only two things are infinite,

the universe and human stupidity,

and I'm not sure about the former.

~ Albert Einstein

Let's approach this issue by looking at several concepts that allow us to work outside the traditional framework of business behavior, to begin to form a picture of what it might look like to develop an organizational version of the Glass Bead Game. In exploring this process, our ability to think "outside the box" and withhold knee-jerk responses becomes a necessary prerequisite for evaluating different concepts—concepts that might catalyze us to move further along the path of increased awareness. Let me begin by restating a few fundamental aspects of dis-ease in the workplace.

First: Most dysfunction in business is destructive to growth and enhanced profitability. *Second:* People caught up in dysfunctional work settings become emotionally and physically sick. When dysfunction takes the form of control and manipulation of behavior through the pursuit of self-centered agendas, humans, as well as systems, pay a big price: they lose a sense of integrity and moral purpose. True, an organization may be profitable and still be dysfunctional. However, there's always a point where dysfunction becomes so dis-eased that the operation starts to inflict much pain on its members.

Some of the victims become numbed by the accumulated de-valuing that takes place, while others suffer a "death of the soul" trying to adapt to unhealthy conditions, losing in the process their integrity and moral self-worth. (As Michael Caine said in the movie Alfie, "Decent clothes ..... a car, but what's it all about??")

It's possible to look at organizational dysfunction solely from a micro-level and to concentrate on reducing the dysfunctions themselves. However, this kind of approach alone won't do much to address the by-products of the globalized market exchange system as a whole.

Thus far, we have seen how turfs, power cliques, authoritarian manage-ment styles, self-serving agendas and defective communication can be

A person must seek his happiness

and inward peace from objects which cannot

be taken away from him.

~ Alexander Humbolt

effectively handled by skilled leaders employing strategies which support group synergy and adherence to common sets of visions. However, once these problems are diminished, we still face a fundamental question: What is the next logical step that needs to be taken?

It's my belief that as organization dysfunction is reduced, efforts must be directed toward defining the ends of the business' purposes as well as determining whose interests are being served. Irradicating dysfunctional behaviors, attitudes and processes in order that a small minority can reap huge benefits while others suffer, should not be an end in itself. We need to continue to develop these humanistic practices and seek ways to provide support and value to all types of shareholders—not just to those who hold huge stock portfolios.

Today's businesses exert enormous influence on how all of us live and work. Business enterprises are entities that have far more control in shaping values than any of us could have ever imagined just a few short decades ago. Having spent a fair bit of time in so-called "successful" companies, I am continually struck by the large numbers of employees whose personal lives are coming apart at the seams.

They are part of the growing number of victims that are subjected to a value structure that is, in and of itself, harmful to one's health and spiritual enrichment. For example, many of today's working men and women aren't able to spend quality time with family and friends; others are engaged in excessive work patterns that result in debilitating stress; there are still others whose distorted sets of priorities lead them into excessive consumption of alcohol or over-the-counter medications.

In my observation, what is so revealing about most jobs is the fact that despite outward signs of success, the majority of employees, regardless of their blue or white collar status, don't seem happy. This is especially true for those who work "on the front lines," as regular

The unconscious wants truth.

It ceases to speak to those who want

something else more than truth.

~ Adrienne Rich

staff or first level supervisors. Most of these workers have very little financial slack, living more or less from paycheck to paycheck.

These are the people for whom the American Dream is always slightly out of reach. Try as they might to "keep up with the Jones'," they find themselves sinking further and further into debt. Many are single parents, who struggle from day to day trying to juggle full time jobs and raise kids at the same time. (On a recent assignment I interviewed a young single mother who was trying to care for her two children. She worked on the company's grave yard shift. These were the only work hours that would allow her to spend time with her children. She made one remark that brought home her personal sacrifice: "A lot of times," she uttered, "I'm so tired that when my kids are home, I fall asleep .... but at least I know I'm there if they need me.") Life is no picnic for these front line soldiers of corporate capitalism.

At the opposite end of this malaise is the world of the corporate executive, a world characterized by exorbitant salaries, lucrative stock options and, if crisis ensues, "golden parachutes," which allow for comfortable exits, if conditions demand. In many ways they, too, are victims—of greed and narrow-mindedness.

What does all this mean? The answer boils down to a question of *values*. Not just material values, but the values contained in issues involving the *quality* of life, of ourselves and those around us.

In raising the issue of dis-ease in the socioeconomic system as a whole, we are treading on delicate turf. One cannot address global socioeconomic structures without consideration of politics and ethics. In this context, I'm not advocating the overthrow of our government or the dissolution of our business structures; rather, I am investigating the implications of introducing a new paradigm, one which offers a different approach to issues such as worker alienation, compensation

The weakness of pure individualism is that there are no pure individuals.

~ Kenneth Boulding

inequities, difficulties involved in attempting to balance home and work life, as well as broader issues concerning the nature of business and the ethics that govern business interests.

These are issues that corporations and small businesses alike should take seriously. To begin to bridge the huge gaps in quality living, not just in our own back yard, but for planet earth as well, we must attempt to design a new form of Glass Bead Game, one that helps us redefine antiquated values and questionable ethics.

It's clear that to reach anywhere near the level of awareness that was achieved through Joseph Knecht's playing of the Glass Bead Game, an effort must be made to move away from "egoistical" thinking toward strategies that provide more altruistic perspectives for business enterprises.

Western societies possess enormous wealth—but it is mostly in the hands of a privileged few. Consequently, the "new" Glass Bead Game must incorporate elements that offer the prospect of new possibilities. To do this, we must first change the level of consciousness about who we are and what drives us to think and act the way we do.

Let's begin with a simple experiment, which you can perform yourself. Here's what is needed: Get an alarm clock. Set it to go off in five minutes. Your assignment is to sit, uninterrupted, in a comfortable upright position, in a quiet setting, doing just one thing: paying attention to your breathing. That's all that's required—just pay attention to the natural pattern of your breath—in and out. Here's the challenging part: if any thoughts or associated images should come to mind, just say to yourself "thinking," and then immediately drop the thought or image and get back to giving your full and complete attention to your breathing. When you've finished this little exercise, go on to the next page and continue reading.

I think I think;

therefore I think I am.

~ Ambrose Bierce

My guess is that most of you experienced difficulty getting through this exercise without a series of thoughts or associated images entering your mind. You may have also experienced difficulty in not "attaching" to some of those thoughts. Further, you may have been surprised by the diverse content of the thoughts or associated feelings you had.

If this was the case, you're not unusual. The vast majority of "normal" people find themselves constantly thinking about past events or future possibilities, while completely neglecting what's going on in the present. Often this kind of thinking is accompanied by feelings or emotions associated with past failures or concern about future outcomes.

The fact of the matter is that none of this thinking is "real" and none of it is what is actually happening in the "now." When we are immersed in "other-time" thinking, not only are we not truly living in the present, we are responding to feelings and emotions that are nothing more than the products of past experiences or future doubts. Simply stated, the past has already happened, and the future is yet to come. So what does that say about the awareness one has in the present moment?

Our relentless experience of these random patterns of thoughts, feelings and emotions that are based on "non-realities," gives credence to a notion that many psychologists maintain—namely, that the functioning mind is quite irrational. Some people express it more bluntly, calling the mind "a drunken monkey." Whatever the label, the fact is, our thought processes are not only random, but are often chaotic as well. The thought processes that hover between past and future also contain a plethora of emotions—fear, anger, sadness, frustration, etc.—which further distort thinking and judgment. This is the first important concept that needs to be understood, as we explore what a "Glass Bead Game" might look like in the workplace.

The world is what we think it is.

If we can change our thoughts,

we can change the world.

~ H.M. Tomlinson

Let's not lose sight of the notion of the random and chaotic nature of our thoughts and related emotions as we look at the next important structural concept. This concept focuses on another way in which we think. It's called "categorization." The concept itself was introduced by a psychologist named Jerome Bruner. Simplified, it goes something like this: When we perceive of a thing, it involves acts of categorization. Given how much information comes at us at any given moment, we try to make sense of it, discarding or ignoring some things, while retaining others.

This, in turn, leads us to try to simplify things by putting thoughts into categories. Some categories are fairly basic, like animals or cars. However, categorization gets more complex when we consider one's values, inherent beliefs or personality traits. As Bruner has stated, "If we come to consider a person as 'aggressive,' we then consistently tend to filter all his/her actions in relation to that category." This leads Bruner to conclude that, "personality traits seem to exist mainly in the category system of the perceiver."

In other words, the experiences we have in the past shape the ways in which we categorize that which we perceive. One might say that both positive and negative experiences strongly influence the categorization process, as do how we feel and react toward things that resemble those experiences.

Bruner further notes that in the presence of a particular stimulus (or incoming "flood" of perceptual data), what is evoked is the category and not the actual occurrence in the external world. Categorization has the potential of weighing a person down with heavy emotional baggage, prejudicial thinking and limited ways of looking at situations.

Applying some of these axioms to business settings, we can grasp a little better the way this form of conditioning can become "afflictive"

Let one therefore keep the mind pure,

for what a man thinks that

he becomes.

~ The Upanishads (900-600 BC)

and hamper both the ability to work effectively with others and in rendering fair judgments and making sound decisions. Because of this categorization phenomenon, deep-seated fears often shape personal defenses, to the degree that people can easily become "ego-centered" and self-serving in their behavior toward themselves and others. It requires focused concentration to plan, manage, direct and influence people, as well as make decisions and judgments that are sound and unbiased. It also takes much disciplined awareness not to bring personal moods or problems into the workplace and to maintain a positive, forward moving attitude while dealing with the emotion-based dis-eases within and around us.

This is why it is so vital to develop greater awareness of how mental processes can distort and negatively influence judgments and decisions, as well as the beliefs we harbor, if we are to build healthier business climates. When our sense of awareness is clouded by fear, doubt, anger and past hurts, it becomes hard to move through life with any real sense of clarity and open-mindedness.

When the heart is fearful and the mind is agitated, ego-based thoughts and actions gain the upper hand. As a result, attitudes and behaviors become distorted. This, in turn, effects the ability to reason and to shape values that are more than just self-serving or protective in nature. Truth be told, most of us are terribly naive about the mental forces that shape our thinking. Because of these factors, the ability to implement plans, think strategically and perform as an effective team player, is often seriously flawed.

It's at this point that we must conclude that any conventional strategic approach to deal with issues in the workplace, such as managing change or dealing with dysfunction, is likely to meet strong resistance due to unresolved, agitated, mental states. This is the primary reason why many expensive and seemingly well thought-out training initia-

The little things?

The little moments?

They aren't little.

~ Jon Kabat-Zinn

tives never fully take hold—or if they are in place, why they rapidly lose their drive and momentum.

The restrictions on our ability to achieve greater mental awareness in how we think and act has led psychologist Claudio Naranjo to conclude that "certain levels of human understanding cannot be claimed ... until the brain can work in more than one way." In the Province of Castilia, the playing of the Glass Bead Game provided that mechanism. So, now, the question becomes, how can we attempt to move toward that same state of mind, one that produces maximum clarity in a framework of non-judgemental thinking?

The answer lies in processes that foster "focused awareness." These processes are known by many names, but they are commonly referred to as "meditative practices." In the words of Dr. Naranjo, these techniques are nothing more than a "persistent effort to detect, and become free from all conditioning, compulsive functioning of mind and body, and habitual emotional responses ...," or, if you will, thought processes that have the power to contaminate states of awareness.

Dr. Robert Ornstein, an authority on meditative practices at the University of California Medical Center, has noted that "the techniques of concentrative meditation are not deliberately mysterious or exotic but are "simply a matter of practical applied psychology." My contention is that by significantly reducing fear-based "noise" that feeds our need to control, avoid or put up barriers of resistance, we are able to become more accepting of uncertainty. Having a "quiet mind" in the midst of stressful, anxiety producing environments creates the potential for acting with increased openness and objectivity.

When "quiet mind" is shared by others in the workplace, dynamic changes in collective perception and awareness become possible. Concurrently, if there is a strong collective intention to critically

Stop thinking that meditation

is anything special.

Stop thinking altogether.

~ Surya Singer

evaluate the ethical practices within an organization, the techniques embodied in enhanced mental awareness techniques are likely to enhance that inquiry.

It has been demonstrated in rigorous scientific experiments that various types meditative practices have the ability to alter both perception and consciousness. To those who are unfamiliar with enhanced techniques for focused awareness, it might seem that I am talking about "brain-washing" or perhaps some form of mysticism with inherent religious connotations. This couldn't be further from the truth.

For decades, western science and medicine have been aware of the powers of "concentrated focus." Dr. Jon Kabat-Zinn, author of *Full Catastrophe Living: Using the Wisdom of Your Body and Mind to Face Stress, Pain, and Illness* has demonstrated how meditative techniques can greatly reduce chronic pain as well as reduce the intensity of various psycho-somatic ailments.

In the book *Healing and the Mind,* based on the TV series developed by Bill Moyers, Dr. Kabat-Zinn notes that:

> *"Meditation is really about learning that the mind constantly chatters. And yet, that chatter winds up being the force that drives us much of the day, in terms of what we do, what we react to and how we feel.... Meditation is a discipline for training the mind to develop greater calm and then to use that calm to bring penetrative insight into our own experience in the moment. From that insight comes greater understanding and, therefore, greater freedom to conduct our lives the way we feel would lead to the greatest wisdom and happiness."*

What we call "meditation" can be employed as an effective tool capable of bringing us closer to the inherent values contained in the

All of the significant battles

are waged within the self.

~ Sheldon Kopp

playing of the Glass Bead Game. By incorporating meditative practice into the work environment, a powerful energy for enhancing the ability to strategically partner is released. Even though the merits of the Strategic Partnering concept outlined earlier are effective, there are many variables dictated by "agitated minds," which dissipate its potential for maximum success.

To illustrate how "agitated minds" negatively impact work environments, let me refer to an experience I had when working with a company to look at their operational strengths and weaknesses: It soon became evident that the training program that this business initiated was not getting through to a majority of its employees. On paper, the training was excellent. But once introduced to staff, its contents were completely lost.

After interviewing dozens of employees, and asking them about the company's training initiative, a number of facts were revealed. Many employees said that sitting for long periods created a sense of restlessness; single mothers were stressed because their child rearing responsibilities were interrupted; supervisors were preoccupied with thoughts about unfinished paperwork, etc.

Several people appeared to be just plain angry about the compulsory nature of the training. It seemed that every person interviewed consciously or unconsciously made reference to thoughts that diverted their attention to the actual training content. The impact of the training was so bad that, for all practical purposes, these sessions could have been held in an empty room, given the degree of attention that was present. Based on the diversity of people in the trainings, I was convinced that this "ignor-ance" of critical concepts was not a product of education, intelligence or job position.

Also apparent was the fact that if these participants had been engaged in on-going meditative awareness practices, their level of attention

Those who seek the truth

by means of intellect and learning

only get further and further

away from it.

~ Huang-Po

would have easily allowed them to absorb and retain the core principles being presented in a fraction of the time allotted. However, without such a tool, their emotions and mental preoccupations held sway. As a result, the content was barely retained, and the buy-in, which was crucial for success, was missing.

Another example of distractions generated by agitated minds involves the behavior of managers at meetings. On countless occasions I've sat in on high level executive meetings representing a variety of different industries. Time after time, I've witnessed people playing all kinds of "one-upsmanship" games, as opposed to listening to arguments and weighing them in a more objective fashion.

At such gatherings, big egos are typically the norm. Meetings like these exemplify a self-centered process of non-communication, whereby each person feels the need to declare the correctness of their views, to the exclusion of the opinions of others. In such instances, not only are people not listening, they have no intention of even trying to listen. Yet these types of encounters occur millions of times each day, in high level meetings, planning sessions, trainings and retreats.

If we even tried to speculate about the amount of time and money that is wasted on such events, the figures would be astounding! Through the use of mental awareness techniques, increased focus on objectives is greatly enhanced. This is because, in the act of calming the mind, the ego's need to lapse into self-centered concerns and protective posturing is significantly diminished. This is a direct result of an expanded sense of inner calm and deeper insight, which accrues from focused concentration.

Meditative techniques have been a tool used by medical practitioners for decades. In the late 1970's, Dr. Carl O. Simonton, a radiation oncologist, had cancer patients practice a form of concentrative medi-

I was going to buy a copy of "The Power of Positive Thinking," and then I thought: "What the hell good would that do?"

~ Ronnie Shakes

tation by having each patient picture, in their "mind's eye," white blood cells attacking cancer cells, much like hungry sharks attacking small fish. Simonton discovered that the patients who were able to develop the most consistent and vivid images seemed to fare noticeably better in treatment. These techniques are still employed today in cancer treatment.

Similarly, the entire field of medical biofeedback is based on the demonstrated fact that the mind can assist in controlling certain physical disorders—high blood pressure and migraine headache being two particularly good examples. All of these practices and procedures that help to control these disorders involve enhanced techniques of mental concentration, similar to those embodied in meditation practices.

Centuries ago, the Roman philosopher Marcus Aurelius noted, "The universe is change; our life is what our thoughts make it." This is true for both the individual and the collective. The ability to engage in Active Dialogue with people whose mental states are clear—without the usual conditioned patterns of fear and denial—offers the potential for a qualitatively new and expansive way of communicating.

With fewer ego-based "hang-ups" present, people in organizational settings are much more likely to carefully explore sensitive issues such as business ethics or global impact, which previously never would have entered the realm of Active Dialogue. In other words, focused awareness techniques are viable tools for enterprises that want to foster more conscious conduct.

There continues to be resistance and skepticism about introducing these techniques into work settings. People are too nervous about change, even if it results in enhanced benefits for everyone. W. H. Auden was correct when he called this modern era "The Age of

The thing always happens that you really

believe in; and the belief in a thing

makes it happen.

~ Frank Lloyd Wright

Anxiety." Today's businesses are, for the most part, defensive and fear driven. Success is often measured only by numbers from one yearly quarter to the next. The manager who is a hero in March may find his head on the chopping block when summer rolls around. Most, if not all, of America's publicly held corporations exist primarily to satisfy only their top shareholders, who have become increasingly more greedy and intolerant of any form of negative cash flow. In this kind of milieu, looking for the right scapegoat to justify downward turns in profitability is not uncommon.

"Business ethics" have, for all practical purposes, become one of the twenty-first century's biggest oxymorons. Today's white collar criminals are now lionized for their philanthropy and secretly honored for their ability to abuse the system and still escape unscathed with a fortune tucked away in Swiss banks.

These behaviors speak of an ideology where there is no right or wrong, good or bad. Situational ethics rule, with winners and losers being the only categories that anyone seriously pays attention to. When a lack of scruples become the order of the day, as they now have, there is a desperate need for a chorus of loud, heroic voices to emerge from within our business ranks and shout in unison, "ENOUGH!!"

Embracing methods of enhanced mental awareness offers a viable framework to give those chosen few the voice they need to begin to change the momentum of what has sadly become an economic system that hurts many more people than it helps.

To validate these sentiments one has only to look at the decrepit state of public education, the treatment of the elderly and the care for the sick and the disadvantaged to understand where this country's emphasis has been placed. There has been of late a movement of

You've got to be very careful

if you don't know where you are going,

because you might

not get there.

~ Yogi Berra

sorts, one that talks about "Spirituality in the Workplace." It has been both widely ignored and grossly misinterpreted. In truth, the notion of "spirit" is not as lofty a concept as many people believe. It merely involves principles that, at first glance, don't appear to be tangible or within easy grasp.

Theoretically, people don't leave their soul behind when they go to work in the morning. (Although many outspoken critics of our current economic system might argue differently!) That's why making the effort to develop concentrative awareness practices in the workplace, in itself, provides a powerful framework for helping people to think and act with greater compassion, while still retaining an interest in growth and profitability.

Once the dimension of "ego control" becomes more balanced, as it often does when serious attention is given to meditative practices, there is a quality of attention and authenticity that becomes a basic part of one's reality. When an aggregate of individuals engages in these practices, especially with the support brought to bare by insightful leadership, the possibility for transformation in values becomes more of a work in progress.

Utilizing the tools of meditation and introducing them to people voluntarily within an organization has the potential for influencing meaningful changes in the way people interact. Once we begin to apply formal approaches to concentrating awareness, the rewards to both individuals and the "public-at-large" will be more than evident.

The ability to "see" things, "in-the-moment," devoid of the emotional and judgmental baggage that typically attaches to thoughts, will release vast amounts of creative questioning about dysfunctional attitudes and behaviors. Most of the time, what appears as complex dysfunctional

In the heating and air conditioning trade,

the point on the thermostat which neither

heating nor cooling must operate, around

72 degrees, is called 'The Comfort Zone'.

It's also known as 'The Dead Zone.'

~ Russell Bishop

situations are often by-products of repressed emotions or unsubstantiated fears from various players within an organizational system.

Let me illustrate this by citing an example involving the behavior of a CEO of a regional utility company I was contracted to work with. This gentleman was described by many critics as a "high paid, do nothing executive." Keeping the status quo intact seemed to be the only policy he ever took seriously. The company's line level workers were basically a well-compensated lot, receiving better than average benefits. However, grumbling and discontent were the norm. It seemed to me that these workers carried with them negatively charged views about their bosses and the other company "higher-ups," due largely to the fact that no real communication between line staff and management existed.

Because of these conditions, seemingly inconsequential events would trigger all manner of negatively charged posturing from both sides of the worker/management barricades. Initially, I experienced difficulty pinpointing exactly what was going on. Then, after careful observation, the picture became abundantly clear. The CEO, it seems, was fearful of any kind of confrontation, especially with lower ranking employees. Because of this, any serious dialogue between individuals and groups about issues that came up was discouraged. Worker complaints went unanswered, decisions were made behind closed doors and attempts to air commonly held grievances were all but outlawed.

This public utility was so obstructed it seemed that at any minute it might implode. As circumstances unfolded, it became obvious that the CEO's fear-based thinking spread downward through the entire management team as a form of informal policy. However, because the company was profitable and nothing ever got too out of hand, his position as head of the company was never threatened. So the fear-based dynamic held sway.

Down in their hearts,

wise men know this truth:

the only way to help yourself

is to help others.

~ Elbert Hubbard

This company lacked any semblance of vitality and vision. Like day-old toast, it was bland and stale. There is no doubt whatsoever that this fear/avoidance-oriented CEO could have benefited enormously from focused awareness practices, as could his managers and line staff. Whatever array of fears he continued to nurture would have been "calmed" through the quieting of his mind. He would also receive an added boost from his key lieutenants because they, too, would be experiencing things from a calmer "inner perspective."

Given this CEO's innate intelligence and curiosity, he could have potentially shaped a highly spirited company—one capable of partnering with employees and the community in all manner of creative pursuits. Unfortunately, his excessive "mental baggage" nixed any possibility that this could become reality. Instead, under his aegis, the company was constantly fighting internal fires—and making fear-based decisions, which kept the outfit in constant tension.

James Allen once said, "As the physically weak man can make himself strong by careful and patient training, so the man of weak thoughts can make them strong by exercising himself in right thinking." Meditative practices, which work on quieting the mind, do just that.

In the playing of Hesse's Glass Bead Game, wisdom spread outward from the Province of Castilia toward the entire country, shaping moral character and articulating the nature of what it meant to be of service. There's a world of difference between a mind-set that is service oriented and one that views control and profitability as the only form of "action matrix."

Because meditative practice reduces the necessity to cling to ego-centered needs, there's a strong likelihood that businesses that embrace these techniques will be more attentive to both service and account-

Be still and cool in your

own mind and spirit.

~ George Fox

ability. This means that both the "internal" and "external" customers—that is, employees as well as consumers—will be served.

Shoshona Zuboff, a Harvard Business School professor, along with her business executive husband James Maxmin, argue in their recent book, *The Support Economy,* that corporations have become far too narcissistic. In addition, they are hung up in antiquated concepts of mass production, to the extent that the idea of really getting close to the customer and serving their needs has all but disappeared from their thinking.

It's easy to recognize this concept being played out. Corporations have become notoriously bad in providing customer service. Granted, there are some notable exceptions. But for the most part, when we make any attempt to call and speak to a human being about a product or service issue, we merely find ourselves getting caught up in a maze of automated telephone menus, with no solution in sight.

The interesting thing is that most consumers have become "numb" in the face of these services lapses, attributing them to just another example of "corporate neglect." Even those companies that appear to recognize the validity of these consumer issues often lack the clarity and intention to address them effectively.

Once again, we are faced with questions of value—this time, the values are focused upon our concepts of self-worth. If we accept the notion that there is more to life and living than the accumulation of wealth and power, then we must be prepared to take a closer look at how businesses operate and who they are really serving. The larger issue is a much more expansive one than merely declaring one system dysfunctional and replacing it with the lesser of two evils. The larger issue is about how to foster and develop a more "humanistic" transformation in ethics and values within our business communities.

Do exactly what you would do

if you felt most secure.

~ Meister Eckhart

This is yet another reason why tools that generate a calmer, more "aware" mind can assist in the process of humanistic transformation. If structured with care and precision, these practices have the power to significantly elevate a company's attentiveness to really serving their customers. In Part Two we explored the kind of leadership characteristics needed to effectively address work-based dysfunction. Many of those leadership characteristics are best carried out when "quiet mind" is present.

There's a term called "dynamic obsolescence" that is often applied to business operations. It means that a product is intentionally produced with only a short life, so that it will need replacing before too long. In other words, certain material items are purposely designed to break down, so new and "better" ones can be purchased. The old expression, "they don't make things like they used to," is right on the money—your money! What is needed, however, is thinking which instead says "let's build this product to last, so that everyone will want one." If you believe this is an ethically sound statement, then we might be talking the same language.

As consumers, what are we to believe? For example, how truthful is business about the products and services that are manufactured and delivered? Again, we are confronted with questions of value—in this instance, the value of telling the truth. To seriously ask these kinds of questions is to speculate about dynamic change. Asking these types of questions is, in effect, acknowledging a willingness to try your hand at playing the Glass Bead Game. Many firms will shy away from such a process because it appears much too threatening to their comfort zones.

During the 1980's, companies discovered the value of having physically fit employees. Some places went so far as to build elaborate fitness centers for their staffs. This trend has continued, albeit somewhat sluggishly. Even though the fitness-in-business trend in still alive, many firms have continued to resist getting on the bandwagon. Statistics tell us that Americans

Earth provides enough

to satisfy every man's need,

but not every man's greed.

~ Mahatma Gandhi

are even more overweight now than they were several years back. This doesn't say much for the success of the fitness-in-business initiative.

The mandate is clear: Companies must consider utilizing effective methods that harmonize human relationships and generate values that foster not just physical well being, but moral and ethical well being. This kind of thinking is not solely local or regional in scope. It includes the well being of all of the world's citizens. Excessive pollution, ecological disintegration and human degradation are not far away from many of our companies' doorsteps.

Albert Einstein noted that, "A man's value to the community primarily depends on how far his feelings, thoughts and actions are directed towards promoting the good of his fellows." Our community has expanded. What we do and how we do it have implications that far exceed the limits of our own small borders. Like it or not, we are now part of a global community. In our efforts to consume, modern man has become a destroyer as well as a producer. And with this destruction has come an attitude of ignor-ance. Unfortunately this attitude has spilled over into developing countries, where exploitation of the strong over the weak continues unabated. It is a global problem—but it's our problem, too.

If we ever needed a "Glass Bead Game," it's now. As much as our churches, synagogues and houses of prayer preach love and peace, we continue to live lives that directly and indirectly promote separation and conflict. In business, individual alienation is a common by-product of shallow work environments. Companies seem to be doing a less than adequate job in addressing these conditions—in fact, arguably, today's modern workplace contributes more problems than solutions to the health of its labor force.

When searching for ways to reverse these harmful conditions, we have to look no further than ourselves. The kind of transformation that we are

I have been a stranger in a strange land.

~ Exodus 2:22

searching for, the one that will have the most lasting impact, doesn't occur rapidly. It must be nurtured. "Practice is the best of all instructions," commented Aristotle centuries before the birth of Christ. He was right.

The first step in the direction of transformation in business involves practicing ways to bring it about. We mustn't wait for perfect solutions because there are none.

The Mechanics of Meditation

What might it look like if a company wanted to take a closer look at utilizing meditative tools? Obviously, it shouldn't be undertaken "piecemeal." People who understand meditative principles AND have a good "feel" for the way organization dysfunction operates are needed as "in-house guides and facilitators."

There are many forms of meditation, meaning there are countless ways that such practices could be realized in the workplace. The form of meditation I'm emphasizing is a natural process of directing attention inward—in essence, focusing concentration away from physical and mental stimuli. The aim is to achieve not just a reduction of stress, but a refinement of thought processes. What is accomplished in the process is a marked reduction in an individual's "mental noise," which is a by-product of accumulated fear, apprehension and conditioned responses.

The idea that a person must sit crossed legged in a lotus position to achieve this state of heightened awareness isn't at all the case. Just a comfortable position on a straight backed chair with both feet on the floor and one hand relaxing in the palm of the other is all that's required. As far as the meditative setting itself, there needs to be a "Quiet Space"—not merely an empty room with desks stacked to one

Meditation is not a means to an end.

It is both the means and the end.

~ J. Krishnamurti

side. Such a space might have soft carpeting, cushions, earth tone colors and perhaps a fountain of some kind with the gentle sound of running water. The potential meditative practitioner might begin to utilize such a space for an undisturbed period of about a half hour or less. However long the meditative period, practice should be consistent and regular. It's essential to build meditation directly into the work day, and not make it just an "add-on" activity.

It's been suggested that while meditating the eyes should be closed; however there are teachers who recommend that the eyes be partially opened, remaining unfocused and gazing ahead on a slight downward angle. Each meditation practitioner needs to play with these techniques to see what feels right for him or her. Focusing on the breath or on the rise and fall of one's chest and abdomen is the classic form of focused attention.

Some meditators find it helpful to count "one" after the first rising and falling of the breath, then "two" after the second rising and falling, proceeding to the number ten, and then repeating the cycle. At first, no matter what methods are employed, one's mind will start to wander. This is quite natural. Just allow the thoughts to come and go, without "clinging" to any of them, as if they were clouds passing overhead. This response applies to emotions as well, many of which might, for an instant, emit a lot of pain or sadness. Once again, don't cling to these things. Allow them to quietly pass.

Be prepared to be interrupted by all kinds of thoughts and images—some may be images of past events long forgotten, while others may be as silly as a theme song you heard while watching a TV commercial. From the sublime to the extreme, your mind will play "drunken monkey." If meditation occurs in the company of others, then one has to become accustomed to lots of contaminating noises: coughing, squirming in seats, etc. Just be aware that these things are going on—once again, no need

All of the masters tell us

the reality of life—which our noisy waking

consciousness prevents us from hearing—

speaks to us chiefly in silence.

~ Karlfried Graf Durckheim

to cling to any of it. Insight meditation is about observation, period. You may have an itch, a slight tension or even some minor pain. If this is the case, it's helpful to try to merely note what's going on and not respond.

While meditating, I try to nurture a sensation that allows me to feel my heart opening, becoming more receptive to all forms of energy from within or without. To assist me in this process I often say to myself "open heart," with each in-breath, and "quiet mind," with each out-breath. After a while, certain words representing concepts that the group wants to focus upon can be used repetitively.

Bear in mind that while meditating, a person is confronting their own unique mental processes, perhaps for the very first time. Rest assured, however, that through practice, patience and a dose of positive thinking, most people will experience some dynamic breakthroughs in their ability to form the kind of "strategic alignments" I was discussing earlier in the book.

Ideally, it would be most helpful to engage an experienced instructor to assist in such sessions—at least until everyone feels comfortable with the techniques and general format. Carrying on these practices at home is very strongly encouraged. Taking even five minutes of uninterrupted time in the evening before retiring, and in the early morning upon awakening, will greatly enhance the progress that can be made in the workplace. In this way, a calmer, more balanced home will be carried synergistically over into the workplace.

It's understood that business settings contain a diverse group of people, personalities and points of view. Some people are compulsive types; others are impatient. Developing meditative practice should be a gentle unfolding for all types of people. No "musts" or "have to's" should be imposed upon anyone. The important thing is for everyone who's meditating to be kind to themselves and not expect too much at the

The journey to happiness

involves finding the courage to go down

into ourselves and take responsibility

for what's there.

All of it.

~ Richard Rohr

outset. Some days will be much better than others. Don't become "discouraged" like those Thai elephants mentioned early in this book.

A Little More About the Mind

It has been noted that beliefs are often formed as a manifestation of experiences, many of them negative, that occurred as far back as early childhood. When the mind gets quiet there is less attachment to these "fixed" viewpoints. Such a state of mind is a prime ingredient for creative expression. This is because the mind is being released from its restrictive bonds. When this experience occurs collectively, "brain-storming" becomes a truly remarkable tool.

Any good business person can immediately see the potential benefits that are within their grasp when meditative practice becomes a fixed part of the work environment. There is no doubt that meditative practice has the capacity to remove obstructive filters, allowing for more expansive views about what is possible. Henry Ford once said, "I am looking for a lot of men who have an infinite capacity to not know what can't be done." Henry, unfortunately, wasn't able to find all that many people who fit this description. If he had introduced meditation to his work force, we might be glided to our destinations at warp speed, without the hassle of traffic jams, for just pennies!

Although that may be a bit of an exaggeration, companies do need people who are truly committed to seeing that goals and objectives succeed. They need individuals who are sincere about their willingness to buy into company-based initiatives. Meditation acts as a "glue" that cements a company's initiatives into a solid foundation for action.

Introducing heightened awareness practices into the workplace allows the collective to more objectively "see" how habits and condi-

We find no real satisfaction in life without obstacles to conquer and goals to achieve.

~ Maxwell Maltz

tioned responses shape attitudes and values. When fear and anxiety are markedly reduced, compassion arises. When an organization becomes compassionate, it moves closer toward a "working understanding" of its greater purpose for existence.

Business needs to recognize that the one of the fundamental aims of meditation is to form a critical mass whose clarity of purpose exerts a positive influence on the direction of the enterprise. Meditative practice in the workplace essentially aims at the integration of values, attitudes and objectives with more "universal" ends of purposes.

As a former therapist, ensconced in western values, I often found myself trying to explain to patients the fact that when thoughts or deep emotions—particularly negative ones—arise, instead of embracing them and becoming victimized, they should try to remain as a "witness" to them, becoming more detached and objective.

At the time, I had very little understanding of the fact that I was actually discussing aspects of meditative practice—without, of course, the religious, cultural or philosophic overtones to which it is often associated. However, if dealing with some of these concepts seems to reflect a call for more "spirituality" in business, I am not at all opposed. The pendulum has swung far too much to the side of exploitation, greed and avarice. It is now time to swing more toward a little "enlightened spirituality."

In the final analysis, it is imperative that we start to think anew about such matters as work, service, compassion and global impact, if we are to exist in a truly healthy world. The responsibility to commit to this kind of thinking needs to transcend the individual and become embodied in the collective. When this happens we will all be the winners in the New Glass Bead Game.

AFTERWORD

Years ago, there was an award winning movie called *The Deer Hunter.* One of the protagonists was a young hunter from a small town in Pennsylvania. After being exposed to the horrors of war and human injustice in Vietnam, he found the act of shooting an animal for sport reprehensible. His insight, developed through shock and trauma, was a sacred respect for the value of life—human and animal.

For many of us, deep insights, such as the one that effected this young man, develop not through shock, but as a result of gradual, incremental processes. After spending years treating people for addictions and working in locked psychiatric wards, I had become somewhat nonchalant to the suffering of others. Mine was a clinical, detached eye. There wasn't room for much emotion. Years later, after I transitioned out of the therapy business, I found myself in the highlands of Guatemala, crossing Lake Atitlan. Relaxing on the deck of the boat, I hardly noticed the strong winds that stirred up the waters and rocked our vessel.

Because we departed early in the morning, I hadn't eaten breakfast. This irritated me. Now, I'd have to wait until we reached our destination, the village of Santiago Atitlan—and who knew the kind of restaurant I might encounter! My stomach started to grumble. I then realized I had placed a loaf of bread in my backpack. Pulling out the bread, I opened my mouth and was about to chomp down on the dry but welcome morsel, when I felt the penetrating gaze of three young girls from the neighboring Tzutuhil village. I smiled in their direction. But they didn't respond. Then I took a closer look. Their eyes were fixed, not on me, but on the bread loaf I held in my hands. Now I understood why they were so focused. They were hungry—very hungry.

Without a second thought, I sprang to my feet and began to quickly distribute the bread to those three hungry waifs. Two of them started devouring it, but the third immediately stood up, ripping hunks from the hands of her two companions. Then, hurriedly, she vanished below deck. I was incensed by her greed and cruelty, in the face of her companions deprivation.

A moment later, she emerged on deck. This time, she was grasping the hand of another Tzutuhil girl. The girl was crippled and had great difficulty walking. They both sat down. I noticed that the crippled youngster was gobbling voraciously the pieces of bread I had distributed only a minute before. Now I understood. The native girl who had ripped the bread forcefully from the hands of her two companions did so in order to feed the one who was left out—the one who could not feed herself.

I could barely contain myself. Tears welled up within me. In that instant, all the world's suffering was sitting across from me on that little Guatemalan skiff. I felt selfish and somewhat guilt ridden. I recalled how ego-centric I had been about my mild state of hunger and how invisible these young Tzutuhils were as I sat, preoccupied with my petty state of discomfort.

I resolved not to permit myself to forget the meaning of this moment. That incident in Guatemala has propelled me to seek tools for lessening the burden of people who are dis-eased. Because my work has been focused in the business arena, I have had many occasions to observe, first hand, workplace dysfunction.

I've come to regard incidents such as the one described above, as "ah-hah" moments—ones that change both perception and perspective. For the Deer Hunter, this "ah-hah" moment was a culmination of cruel and violent acts in combat which allowed him to come face-to-face with an understanding of how precious life is, and how quickly and arbitrarily it can be taken away.

In large measure, attempting to generate an acceptance for positive change in business and organizational settings is about helping people experience their own form of "ah-hah!" moments.

The author Herman Melville once reflected: "We cannot live only for ourselves. A thousand fibers connect us with our fellow men; and along those fibers, as sympathetic threads, our actions run as causes, and they come back to us as effects." Let our actions in the workplace and beyond be ones that encourage fairness and mutually shared abundance; let them promote a sense of active curiosity about how we, as individuals, can best serve others. In serving others, we nourish ourselves........ "ah-hah!!"

References

Bolt, Laurence G. *Zen Soup*. New York: Penguin Group, 1997

Cooney, Barry. "Touching the Masculine Soul" in *Wingspan: Inside the Men's Movement*, Christopher Harding, Editor, p.36, New York: St. Martin's Press, 1992

Dalai Lama, His Holiness. *Ethics for the New Millennium*. New York: Riverhead Books, 1999

Fenchuk, Gary W. *Timeless Wisdom*. Virginia: Cake Eaters, Inc.,1998

Fritz, Robert. *The Path of Least Resistance*. New York: Fawcett Columbine Books, 1989

Katzenbach, Jon R. and Smith, Douglas K. *The Wisdom of Teams*. Boston: Harvard Business School Press, 1993

Maxwell, John C. *Developing the Leader Within You*. Tennessee: Thomas Nelson, Inc., 1993

Millman, Dan. *The Laws of Spirit*. California: H.J. Kramer, 1995

Moyers, Bill. *Healing and the Mind.* New York: Doubleday, 1993

Nachmanovich, Stephen. *Free Play.* Los Angeles: Jeremy P. Tarcher Inc., 1990

Naranjo, Claudio and Ornstein, Robert E. *On the Psychology of Meditation.* New York: Viking Press, 1992

Peters, Tom. *In Pursuit of Wow!* New York: Vintage Books, 1994

Roger-John and McWilliams, Peter. *Do It!* Los Angeles: Prelude Press, 1991

Slater, Robert. *29 Leadership Secrets from Jack Welch.* New York: McGraw Hill 2003

Notes

Notes

Notes

Notes

Jade Bear Publications

BOOK ORDER FORM

Conquering Dysfunction in the Workplace:
Three Winning Strategies to Bring New Life to Troubled Work Environments

by Barry Cooney, Ph.D.

$19.95 each

Quantity Discounts: 5 or more copies - 10% reduction
10 or more copies - 20% reduction
25 or more copies - 25% reduction

Shipping and Handling: $1.00 for each book ordered.

Please send your name, address and check or money order payable to:

Jade Bear Publications
1704-B Llano Street, Suite 244
Santa Fe, New Mexico 87505

* *

Barry Cooney, Ph.D.
is available for Workshops, Seminars, Consultation Projects
and Public Speaking Engagements.

To contact him, please phone or email:

Within New Mexico, USA: 505-474-0515
Toll Free: 888-474-0515
E-mail: bcooney779@aol.com

Thank You for Your Interest !!